CHICAGO PUBLIC LIBRARY
AVALON BRANCH
8148 S. STONY ISLAND AVENUE
CHICAGO, IL 60617

THE MILWAUKEE ROAD

TOM MURRAY

MBI

Dedication

To my mother, Mary L. Murray, who taught me that it's better to see the glass as half full, rather than half empty.

First published in 2005 by MBI, an imprint of MBI Publishing Company, Galtier Plaza, Suite 200, 380 Jackson Street, St. Paul, MN 55101-3885 USA

© Tom Murray, 2005

All rights reserved. With the exception of quoting brief passages for the purposes of review, no part of this publication may be reproduced without prior written permission from the Publisher.

The information in this book is true and complete to the best of our knowledge. All recommendations are made without any guarantee on the part of the author or Publisher, who also disclaim any liability incurred in connection with the use of this data or specific details.

This publication has not been prepared, approved, or licensed by Canadian Pacific Railway. We recognize, further, that some words, model names, and designations mentioned herein are the property of the trademark holder. We use them for identification purposes only. This is not an official publication.

MBI titles are also available at discounts in bulk quantity for industrial or sales-promotional use. For details write to Special Sales Manager at MBI Publishing Company, Galtier Plaza, Suite 200, 380 Jackson Street, St. Paul, MN 55101-3885 USA.

ISBN-13: 978-0-7603-2072-3
ISBN-10: 0-7603-2072-1

Edited by Dennis Pernu
Designed by Christopher Fayers

Front cover: On the front cover: MILW 205, and SD40-2, helps haul train 201 near Homer, Minnesota, on September 15, 1985. *Steve Glischinski*

Frontis: The Super Dome, from a 1956 promotional booklet. *Author collection*

Title page: Despite a surge in traffic in the early 1970s following the Burlington Northern merger, by 1979 traffic on The Milwaukee Road's Puget Sound extension was down to one train daily in each direction. On May 31, 1979, westbound train 201 is in Sixteen Mile Canyon at Lombard, Montana, powered by two SD40-2s, an MP15AC, and an SD10. *Phil Mason*

Back cover: The Milwaukee's flagship electric motive power from 1951 until the end of electrified operations in 1974 was the group of 12 streamlined, double-ended units commonly known as "Little Joes." This eastbound freight is preparing to depart Avery with Joes E77 and E75 and GP9 321 in September 1972. *Phil Mason* **Inset:** The Chicago Railroad Fair coincided with the delivery of the final cars to streamline the *Olympian Hiawatha*, including the Skytop Lounge cars (which also went into service on the *Hiawathas* between Chicago and the Twin Cities). The Milwaukee produced this illustration to promote both the fair and the new equipment. *Author collection.*

Printed in China

Contents

Acknowledgments 6

Introduction 7

Chapter 1   Midwestern Roots *12*

Chapter 2   Reaching the Pacific *26*

Chapter 3   Between Two World Wars *46*

Chapter 4   World War II and the Transition from

Steam to Diesel *58*

Chapter 5   Passenger Service *76*

Chapter 6   Modernizing the Railroad:

The 1950s and 1960s *96*

Chapter 7   The Final Years: 1970-1985 . . . . *120*

Sources *158*

Index *159*

Acknowledgments

It should be obvious to anyone who looks at this book that it was not a solo project. I am indebted to all of those who have helped make it a reality.

First, there are the many authors who have already written about The Milwaukee Road. Among them, two in particular warrant special mention. August Derleth, though he wrote only a single book about the Milwaukee—its centennial history, published in 1948—provided a wellspring on which subsequent writers have drawn, including me. Jim Scribbins spent more than four decades as an employee of the railroad, and has written four volumes that belong on the bookshelf of any follower of the Milwaukee. I was fortunate to have those books available to me as I wrote this one. Jim also read the manuscript as it was being developed and provided valuable suggestions and corrections. Thank you, Jim.

Some will pick up this book primarily so that they can look at the photographs. I can understand that. I was fortunate to have more than a dozen fine photographers contribute their work to this project: Bob Anderson, Eric Blasko, Mike Cleary, Mike Foley, Dave Gayer, Steve Glischinski, Phil Gosney, John Leopard, Phil Mason, Joe McMillan, Steve Patterson, Jim Scribbins, Don Sims, and Stan Smaill. I had to be very selective about the material I was able to use, given the space limitations of a book like this, but I hope they will feel that their photos have been treated well.

Archival photographs were also important in telling this story. I would like to thank the staffs of the Milwaukee Road Archives at the Milwaukee Public Library and the Wisconsin Historical Society for granting me access to their collections and for allowing their materials to be used here. Sue Mobley of the Milwaukee Road Archives was especially helpful in locating and making available materials from that vast collection.

The California State Railroad Museum also assisted by allowing the reproduction of several photographs from the collection of Philip R. Hastings, M.D., which was donated to the museum by his family in 1997.

To help keep this story focused and accurate, I asked several Milwaukee Road veterans to read it in draft form and provide their comments and suggestions. Aside from Jim Scribbins, this group included Gordon Jonasson, Gene Knol, and Larry Long. Each of them made an important contribution to this project. Another Milwaukee veteran, John Grube, provided significant details about construction methods at the Milwaukee Shops. Michael Sol read a draft of the first three chapters of the book and provided valuable comments about the railroad's early history. However, I take full responsibility for this book's factual accuracy and for the soundness of its interpretations; any errors or oversights that have survived the review process are mine alone.

Doing this book gave me an opportunity to get reacquainted with another Milwaukee Road alumnus, Wally Abbey. He directed the railroad's corporate communications efforts from 1975 to 1980. Wally kindly shared with me several items from his personal archives, which helped me get a better understanding of the company's final years.

The Milwaukee Road Historical Association (MRHA) also deserves mention for being in the forefront of groups devoted to preserving the historical record of a particular railroad. Their quarterly journal, *The Milwaukee Railroader*, is among the finest publications of any such group, and is well worth the attention of anyone with an ongoing interest in The Milwaukee Road.

Finally, I want to thank my wife, Marcia. She didn't simply tolerate my work on this project—she supported it from start to finish.

INTRODUCTION

MILW 137 and another unit have helped train 201 to Roland, at the west end of St. Paul Pass Tunnel, and the crew is now preparing to run light to Avery, in June 1979. *Phil Mason*

Few railroads have attracted as loyal a following as The Milwaukee Road. The railroad ceased to exist as an independent company in 1985, yet its memory continues to be perpetuated by those who worked for it, rode its trains, were affected by it through family or personal connections, or simply admired it.

Though it was closely identified with the city of Milwaukee and the state of Wisconsin, the railroad played an important role in the economies of all the states of the Upper Midwest. Its roots were as a granger road but it was a critical ingredient in the emergence of Milwaukee, St. Paul, and other cities as centers of manufacturing and trade.

As a passenger carrier, the Milwaukee forged an identity as strong as that of any railroad, particularly following the inauguration of the high-speed *Hiawathas* between Chicago and the Twin Cities in the mid-1930s.

Part of the railroad's appeal was in the fact that it put on a different face than its rivals. Much of its equipment—locomotives, as well as passenger and freight cars—was home-grown, built at the company's Milwaukee shops using its own distinctive designs.

For most of the twentieth century, the Milwaukee played the role of underdog. It was surrounded by more prosperous railroads, but it justified its existence by providing competitive service at low cost. Nothing better demonstrated The Milwaukee Road's grit and determination in the face of its competitors' economic power than its 1905 decision to build its own line to Puget Sound. The high

engineering standards and partial electrification of the western extension were symbolic of the Milwaukee's conviction that it could effectively compete with the Hill lines—Great Northern (GN) and Northern Pacific (NP)—for transcontinental freight and passenger traffic.

Prior to World War II, the Milwaukee twice sought the protection of the bankruptcy laws, in 1925 and again in 1935. Both times, it reorganized and continued to operate without substantial changes to its route map. The postwar world brought new opportunities for the company, but also new challenges, particularly in the form of the interstate highway system, which allowed truckers to compete for the railroad's most profitable

Milwaukee E71 leads four diesels into Alberton, Montana, in August 1973. *Steve Patterson*

The *Olympian Hiawatha* pauses at Butte, Montana, in March 1953. *Don Sims*

freight business. The automobile, as well as the burgeoning airline system, siphoned away much of its passenger traffic.

As the number of independent railroads began to shrink through merger and consolidation, Milwaukee Road management made efforts to find a home for the company. If the fates had willed it, the Milwaukee could have joined either with rival Chicago & North Western (C&NW) or with the connecting Canadian National/Grand Trunk Western system. But both of these efforts failed. In fact, The Milwaukee Road never participated in the modern merger movement; its route map of the mid-1970s was little changed from that of 50 years earlier. The Milwaukee Road was, plain and simple, The Milwaukee Road.

Ultimately, the strong will of its management, the dedication if its employees, and the uniqueness of its identity were not enough to make The Milwaukee Road a success as a business enterprise. Though the company is remembered today primarily for its trains, its equipment, and its electrification, the fact is that these assets had to make money in order to be continually renewed, updated, and upgraded. In the West, decades of playing David to the Goliath represented by the Hill lines took their toll. On the eastern half of the railroad, an overbuilt granger network sapped the company's resources. In the final analysis, there was too much railroad, too little traffic, and, under the regulatory regime of the era, little opportunity to correct this imbalance.

GN, NP, and their jointly controlled Chicago, Burlington & Quincy and Spokane, Portland & Seattle came together as Burlington Northern in 1970. The Milwaukee picked up new traffic as a result of merger-related conditions, but because of deferred maintenance, its physical plant was not up to the task of handling this business. In late 1977, it went into bankruptcy for a third time. By 1981 it had shrunk to a "core" railroad, absent the western extension, and in early 1985 the company's remaining rail assets were acquired by competitor Soo Line.

Today, many followers of the Milwaukee continue to ask why those responsible for the company—its management, its shareholders and creditors, its bankruptcy trustees, its regulators, and the court responsible for overseeing the company in its final years—made the decisions they did, and whether the Milwaukee might have been able to survive in some form if different decisions had been made. Those are important questions, and they deserve the best answers that serious scholarship can provide, but such research lies outside the scope of this book.

What this book does provide is an overview of the company's history as a railroad and as a business. It attempts to show how the Milwaukee carried out its mission to serve the shipping and traveling public over the course of its 135-year history. If this volume inspires others to carry out further research into the history of The Milwaukee Road, then it will have served its purpose.

SD40-2 28 was purchased in 1973 for service on Lines West, but by 1984, when this photo was taken at Bensenville, Illinois, it was in general freight service on the company's remaining core network. A mechanical department employee is adding sand to the unit, part of the locomotive servicing routine at every engine terminal.
Eric Blasko

After the February 1980 embargo of many western route-miles, the Milwaukee kept its Montana Line as far as Miles City, plus two branches, including Milbank to Sisseton, South Dakota. In 1982 the Sisseton Branch was sold to the Sisseton Line Association and operated by Dakota Rail, Inc., from 1982 to 1987; by Sisseton Southern Railway from 1987 to 1989; and, beginning in 1989, by Sisseton-Milbank Railroad, owned by shippers, bankers, and area farmers. Here, the Sisseton Patrol at Wilmot, South Dakota, is powered by SDL39 585, in December 1981. Milwaukee operations west of Ortonville, Minnesota, ended on March 31, 1982. *Steve Glischinski*

CHAPTER ONE

MIDWESTERN ROOTS

When Wisconsin became a state in 1848, it had many natural advantages that boded well for its future prosperity. It was situated between Lake Michigan to the east, the Mississippi River to the west, and Lake Superior to the north. Two major river systems, the Fox running northeastward and the Wisconsin to the southwest, provided low-cost means of transportation for riverside communities.

Lead deposits in the southwestern part of the state produced a commodity that would be much in demand in the industrializing

economy of the United States. Climate and soil in the south and west were favorable for raising crops, particularly wheat. Forests in the north and east provided an ample supply of lumber. However, the state's internal river systems did not have the geographic reach to support commercial mining and agricultural needs. The Mississippi, as valuable as it was to Wisconsin and other states as an avenue of commerce, was not an efficient way to reach eastern markets like New York and Boston.

What Wisconsin needed was a transportation system that would go where its designers wanted it to, not where nature took it. Canals were considered but, as in many other states, they never developed into a significant form of commerce. Plank roads came into use starting in the late 1840s, but they were a poor answer to the need for long-distance transportation. The state needed a railroad.

The Farmer's Railroad

In 1849, work began on the Milwaukee & Waukesha Railroad Company. In 1850, the Milwaukee & Waukesha was renamed, becoming the Milwaukee & Mississippi Railroad Company (M&M). By November 1850, five miles of the planned 20-mile route had been completed and the first train operated. Three months later the line reached Waukesha, and on February 25, 1851, the first train operated along the entire route.

However, by this time, it had become clear to everyone that a railroad to Waukesha was only the beginning. The explosive growth in the state's population—from 35,000 people in 1840 to 310,000 ten years later—demanded better transportation. Financing of the initial few miles of the railroad was handled through a barter system, but soon the railroad's backers realized that cash was the only acceptable

SD40-2s 158 and 146 lead Milwaukee train 250 over a segment of Davenport, Rock Island & North Western trackage rights at Princeton, Iowa, in January 1985. *John Leopard*

Previous page: The original six-car *Hiawatha* consist is shown behind Alco 4-4-2 No. 1. *Milwaukee Road photo, author collection*

Wisconsin's oldest surviving railroad depot, built in 1857, is this structure at Mineral Point, seen here circa 1890. Built with 2-foot-thick limestone blocks, the building was restored beginning in 1999. CM&StP 4-4-0 280 was an 1873 product of Grant Locomotive Works of Paterson, New Jersey, and was originally Western Union Railroad No. 33, *Burlington*. CM&StP acquired the Western Union in 1879. *Wisconsin Historical Society/Image WHi-24906*

form of exchange for one very important item that had to come from outside the state: rails. As Milwaukee Road historian August Derleth tells the story, the mayor of the town of Milton told the company's directors, "See here; I can mortgage my farm for $3,000, and go east, where I came from, to get the money for it. Now, are there not one hundred men between Milwaukee and Rock River that can do the same? If so, here is your money." The plan proved successful beyond anything the mayor could have imagined. According to Derleth, by 1857 roughly 6,000 farmers had mortgaged their properties to purchase the stock of various railroad companies, including that of the Milwaukee & Mississippi. Over time, the mortgages found their way into the hands of eastern financiers.

Most prominent among the builders of the line was Milwaukee civic leader Byron Kilbourn. A company history would later describe him as "one of three men who virtually owned Milwaukee in the mid-1830s." He became mayor of Milwaukee in 1848 and president of the railroad in 1849.

The railroad's first financial crisis came very early in its life. In April 1851, the same month that regular service began between Milwaukee and Waukesha, the company found itself unable to pay interest on its debt. The M&M, which was steadily extending its sights westward, was the victim of irregularities in the sale of its bonds. It made a settlement with bondholders in the amount of $14,518, a considerable sum for the infant company. Kilbourn was quoted as saying that

Kilbourn, Wisconsin, named for Byron Kilbourn, one of the pioneers of railroad organization and construction in Wisconsin, was where the La Crosse & Milwaukee crossed the Wisconsin River. Its scenic attractions made it an early focus of the railroad's efforts to attract passenger business. In 1931, the city of Kilbourn changed its name to "Wisconsin Dells." Photographer H. H. Bennett made many photographs in the area, including this one of a CM&StP train crossing the Wisconsin River. *Wisconsin Historical Society/Image WHi-7994*

this transaction "came very near ruining the company entirely." The incident led to a falling out between Kilbourn and the company's board, and to his removal as president in 1851.

In 1853, the first locomotive built in Wisconsin (at the Menomonee Foundry in Milwaukee) had been placed into service on the M&M. The railroad's cars were also being constructed in Milwaukee, as they would be for more than 100 years. At the end of 1854, the company had a total of 22 locomotives, 7 passenger cars, 4 baggage cars, 201 covered and 50 uncovered freight cars, 40 gravel cars, and 14 hand cars. By this time, the railroad had been extended from Waukesha to Madison by way of Eagle and Milton, a total of 97 miles, some of which represented the extra miles needed to serve the towns of influential stakeholders. A more direct line between Milwaukee and Madison (via Watertown and Sun Prairie), completed in 1869, would shorten the distance by 17 miles.

The next objective as the company moved westward was to fulfill the geographic promise inherent in its name, by reaching the Mississippi at Prairie du Chien, approximately 100 miles west of Madison. It did so in April 1857. But the Panic of 1857 brought a widespread decline in economic activity. Shipments of both agricultural products and manufactured goods declined dramatically. The Milwaukee & Mississippi cut expenses in the hope of averting bankruptcy. Derleth

Above: West of Tomah, Wisconsin, builders of the La Crosse & Milwaukee encountered a ridgeline necessitating the construction of a tunnel. The first bore was completed in 1858, but proved unstable. A second, brick-lined tunnel was completed just to the north in 1876. Here, construction workers pose at the east portal of the new tunnel. Chicago & North Western constructed a third tunnel, north of the two shown here; it collapsed in 1973, after which C&NW used the Milwaukee's tunnel. *Wisconsin Historical Society/Image WHi-24918* Below: The Milwaukee & Mississippi reached Milton, Wisconsin, in the fall of 1852. From Milton, lines were built northwest to Madison and south to Janesville. Here, SD7 505 powers a local freight through Milton Junction in the 1960s. *Don Sims*

writes that by 1859, "certain sections of the road needed repair badly . . . [and] some portions needed a complete renewal."

In 1860, the company went into bankruptcy after defaulting on its mortgages, and in January 1861 a new company, the Milwaukee & Prairie du Chien Railway Company (backed by New York financiers), was organized to purchase the assets of the Milwaukee & Mississippi.

Rotary snowplows are often thought of as mountain machines, but the rolling topography of north-central Iowa required railroad builders to use cuts, which filled up with compacted snow during the worst storms. This January 1982 photo shows rotary X900215 working on the Calmar-to-Lawler line. Opened in 1869, this segment eventually formed part of the Milwaukee's line to Rapid City, South Dakota. *Photo by Philip Hastings, courtesy of California State Railroad Museum/negative no. 3156*

Events of the next few years would put control of Wisconsin's first railroad back into the hands of local interests, but not without some pain for the farmers who had been the company's original source of capital. As the easterners who had come into possession of the farm mortgages began to foreclose on the mortgaged properties, the farmers, threatened with the loss of their properties, accused the railroad developers of fraud. The Wisconsin legislature passed a series of laws aimed at preventing the foreclosures, each of which was struck down by the courts. Eventually the M&M reached a settlement with the farmers, who in turn made agreements with the mortgage holders to prevent further foreclosures. This series of events turned many in the state against the railroads.

Alexander Mitchell, a Scotsman who had come to Milwaukee in 1839 and gained prominence in the young city's financial affairs, was responsible for the reversion of the Milwaukee & Mississippi to local control and would go on to play a dominant role in Wisconsin railroading for more than two decades. Mitchell had been a director of the M&M from 1849 to 1855 and in 1858. He was a financier who believed that Wisconsin's economic interests, including its transportation network, could best be protected under the control of the state's own citizens. The aftermath of the Panic of 1857, by weakening the original stockholders' hold on the state's railroads, would give him that opportunity.

Byron Kilbourn, who had been removed as president of the Milwaukee & Mississippi, in 1853 became the first president of another pioneer Wisconsin railroad, the La Crosse & Milwaukee, which was building northwestward across the state. The company secured land grants to finance its construction, but it soon became public knowledge that Kilbourn had bribed the governor and other officeholders in order to get the grants, and in 1857 he lost control of the company. In 1858 and 1859, the La Crosse & Milwaukee defaulted on its bonds and a bankruptcy trustee was appointed. In 1863 the Milwaukee & St. Paul Railway (M&StP) was organized under Mitchell's leadership to acquire the La Crosse & Milwaukee.

The station of Buena Vista, Iowa, was on the Mississippi River, about 25 miles north of Dubuque. This portion of the railroad was completed in 1871. *Wisconsin Historical Society/ Image WHi-8129*

Milwaukee train 251, a Bensenville, Illinois-to-Muscatine, Iowa, run, crosses the Mississippi River from Savanna, Illinois, to Sabula, Iowa, in September 1979. A summer ferry and winter ice crossing were used to transfer cars across the Mississippi until the present swing bridge between Savanna and Sabula was completed in 1881. *John Leopard*

Mitchell expanded his role in the state's rail system by becoming a director (in 1866) and president (in 1867) of the Milwaukee & Prairie du Chien Railway Company. The state's two major railroads were now under common control by the Milwaukee & St. Paul. According to Derleth, the merged company had 820 miles of track, 125 locomotives, 74 passenger cars (including 6 sleeping cars), and 2,248 freight cars of various types. It also owned 80 acres of land in the city of Milwaukee.

An 1868 map of the company shows the following major routes:

- Milwaukee to Minneapolis via Waukesha, Milton, Madison, and Prairie du Chien, Wisconsin; McGregor, Calmar, and Cresco, Iowa; and Austin, Owatonna, Faribault, and Mendota, Minnesota (408 miles);
- Milwaukee to La Crosse, Wisconsin, via Watertown, Columbus, Portage, New Lisbon, Tomah, and Sparta (196 miles);
- Milwaukee to Portage, Wisconsin, via Granville, Iron Ridge, and Horicon, the original route of the La Crosse & Milwaukee (95 miles);
- Milton to Monroe, Wisconsin, via Janesville (42 miles);
- Watertown to Sun Prairie, Wisconsin (26 miles); and
- Horicon to Berlin and Winneconne, Wisconsin (58 miles).

Derleth notes that "by the end of 1869, the Milwaukee & St. Paul controlled every through route in Wisconsin from the lake shore to the Mississippi, finally fulfilling the

With the completion of the iron bridge at La Crosse, Wisconsin, in 1876, the CM&StP was able to offer single-line service between Chicago and the Twin Cities via Portage and La Crosse. *Wisconsin Historical Society/Image WHi-24910*

dreams of the directors of the old Milwaukee & Mississippi."

Though the company dominated the state, it did not have a monopoly. The Chicago & North Western had penetrated into Wisconsin as far as Green Bay. Mitchell briefly served as president of both the M&StP and the C&NW, but the companies did not consolidate and he soon gave up the C&NW post. Until it could complete its own line to Chicago, however, the M&StP depended on the C&NW to reach that city.

Chicago and St. Paul: Becoming a Trunk Line

The early 1870s were years of rapid growth for the Milwaukee & St. Paul. In January 1872, the company acquired the St. Paul & Chicago Railway Company, which had been building a line along the western bank of the Mississippi since 1869. This would eventually form part of The Milwaukee Road's mainline between Chicago and the Twin Cities.

In early 1873, the M&StP opened its own line to Chicago, and in February 1874 the company's name was changed to reflect this fact, becoming Chicago, Milwaukee and St. Paul Railway Company. It would retain this name until 1928. By the end of 1874, the CM&StP had 1,399 route miles.

The railroad's focus was now on expanding westward. In northwestern Iowa, the company proceeded westward from Mason City toward the Dakota Territory. In the southern part of Iowa, construction crews progressed from Sabula Junction (across the Mississippi River from Savanna, Illinois) toward Marion, roughly halfway to the eventual goal of Omaha. Another line pushed in a northwesterly direction from Davenport toward Monticello and Delaware.

Two companies that would subsequently come under CM&StP ownership were engaged in building into the portion of the Dakota Territory that would, in 1889, become South Dakota. One of these companies reached Yankton in 1873; another reached Sioux Falls in 1878. The CM&StP also built into the state on its own, reaching Canton and Marion Junction in 1879. In Minnesota, a major accomplishment of the 1870s was the completion of an east-west line across the southern part of the state, through Albert Lea.

In the mid-1870s, two key bridges opened across the Mississippi River, replacing ferry operations. One was between Prairie du Chien, Wisconsin, and North McGregor (later Marquette), Iowa. This bridge employed a novel pontoon design that could swing out of the way to permit river traffic to proceed. Ramps connected to the pontoon section allowed trains to use the bridge regardless of the level of the river. This bridge remained in service until 1961. In 1876, the railroad's direct line from Milwaukee to St. Paul was completed with the construction of an iron bridge between La Crosse, Wisconsin, and La Crescent, Minnesota.

The Chicago, Milwaukee & St. Paul reinforced its dominance of east-west routes between Lake Michigan, north of Chicago, and the Mississippi River with the 1879 acquisition of a line from Racine, Wisconsin, to Savanna, Illinois, on the Mississippi River. The following year, it acquired another Savanna route, this one from Chicago. By 1880, the CM&StP and its constituent lines totaled 3,894 miles, more than double the mileage of ten years earlier. Mileage figures by state or territory were:

Wisconsin	1,208
Iowa	1,037
Minnesota	996
Dakota	364
Illinois	122

The satisfaction that Alexander Mitchell and the rest of the company's management could take in the steady expansion of the railroad was tempered by the emergence of forces that sought to control and constrain the economic power of the CM&StP and other railroads. In the late 1860s and early 1870s, the Grange movement had begun as a vehicle for farmers to express their displeasure with rail rates and rules. In 1874, the Potter Law was passed in Wisconsin establishing a railroad commission empowered to set rates for rail freight and passenger service. Though upheld by the U.S. Supreme Court, the law proved to be a paper tiger. Derleth writes that "the reduction in rates demanded by the Potter Law did not actually work such a hardship on the railroads as was at first contemplated." It was soon repealed by the Wisconsin legislature, but this and similar laws in other states foreshadowed the passage of the Interstate Commerce Act by the U.S. Congress in 1887.

CM&StP Class H6d 4-4-0 723 was an 1887 product of Cooke Locomotive Works of Paterson, New Jersey. Shown here in an undated photo at Milwaukee, it was renumbered 563 in 1899 and 513 in 1912, and scrapped in 1927. *Milwaukee Road Archives of the Milwaukee Public Library*

Origins of "The Milwaukee Road"

"The Milwaukee Road" was not adopted as part of the railroad's logo until 1953, and it was never the company's formal legal name. Nevertheless, it has a long history as a nickname applied both by the public and by the company's own management and employees. Milwaukee Road historian Michael Sol explains the lineage this way:

As railroads began expansion in Wisconsin, the usage was common: the "Milwaukee" was the Milwaukee & Mississippi, just as its competitor, the La Crosse & Milwaukee was the "La Crosse" road. As the Milwaukee & Mississippi morphed into the Milwaukee & Prairie du Chien, and the La Crosse was reorganized into the Milwaukee & St. Paul, the first company continued to be referred to as "the Milwaukee", and the second, interestingly, as "the La Crosse", then gradually, the "St. Paul" road. In 1867, when Alexander Mitchell merged the Milwaukee & Prairie du Chien and the Milwaukee & St. Paul together into the Milwaukee & St. Paul, correspondence from the era consistently refers to the "new" company as "the Milwaukee." However, the "St. Paul" nickname of the Milwaukee & St. Paul also continued in usage. In financial circles the new company was consistently known as "the St. Paul."

When it emerged from bankruptcy in 1928, the company's corporate name was "Chicago, Milwaukee, St. Paul and Pacific Railroad Company." In that year the words "The Milwaukee Road" began to appear on timetables and other company publications. In 1953, the shorter nickname replaced the full corporate name in the company's red tilted-rectangle logo. This book follows the convention of capitalizing all three words—The Milwaukee Road—just as the company did in its logo from 1953 to 1985.

Extensions to the Missouri River

In the 1880s, the CM&StP continued to expand its geographic reach. Derleth quotes a *Milwaukee Sentinel* piece about the railroad's "car famine" early in the decade, in which it was claimed that the railroad was "1,000 cars short of their present requirements west of the Mississippi."

The CM&StP contributed to, and benefited from, the development of the region. It became a holder of large blocks of real estate, which were managed with an eye toward putting traffic on the railroad. By 1881, this had become such an important function that a separate subsidiary, the Milwaukee Land Company, was formed to manage this aspect of the company's affairs. It also bought coal deposits at Braceville, Illinois, and Oskaloosa, Iowa, to provide fuel for its locomotives.

At the beginning of the decade, the company had three specific cities in mind as targets for its growing network: Fargo, Kansas City, and Omaha. Fargo was reached in 1884. Kansas City was attained by completion of a line from Ottumwa, Iowa, in 1887.

To gain access to Omaha, the company considered building a bridge across the Missouri River from Council Bluffs, Iowa (which the CM&StP had reached in 1882), but by 1890 it had negotiated an agreement with Union Pacific for trackage rights over that company's bridge and into Omaha's Union Passenger Station.

Mid-decade saw significant changes in the company's leadership. S. S. Merrill, who had served as general manager under Mitchell, died in 1885 and was replaced by Roswell Miller. Mitchell died on April 19, 1887, and Miller became president of the company. Derleth summarizes the changes in the company during Mitchell's tenure: "The road, which had begun with a loose network of small lines drawn together by Mitchell with Milwaukee as a central terminus, was now a great web of rails spread over five states and the Dakota territory, with the central terminus of the road gradually shifting to Chicago."

In addition to the death of Alexander Mitchell, who had been president of the company for almost 22 years, the year 1887 brought to a close one phase of the CM&StP's expansion, though the company would continue to grow in size over the next two decades. The annual report for 1887 listed lines completed during the year totaling 182.2 miles. With the completion of these lines, the report said, "all new construction was practically finished at the close of the year, and no new work has since been authorized or undertaken by the Company."

At year-end, the CM&StP had a total of 5,669.95 miles of main track, of which all but 8.52 miles was owned solely by the company. The railroad owned 740 locomotives; 375 passenger cars (coaches and sleeping, parlor, and dining cars); 233 baggage, mail, and express cars; 14,312 boxcars; 7,201 stock, flat, coal, and refrigerator cars; and 510 cabooses and wrecking and tool cars.

A major theme of the company's annual report was that its trackage, equipment, bridges, and other infrastructure were owned outright except for mortgages. This emphasis on freedom from alliances and encumbrances was a principal legacy of the Mitchell years and one element in the CM&StP's reputation as a carrier that went its own way, irrespective of what its competitors might do.

A pair of GP38-2s power Milwaukee train 255 past a country store at Winona, Minnesota, in July 1981. This route, between La Crescent, Minnesota, and St. Paul, was laid out by the St. Paul & Chicago Railway between 1869 and 1872. *John Leopard*

Boxcab helper E45A and its mates have been cut in mid-train as they assist an eastbound train to the top of the grade at Pipestone Pass, Montana, in August 1973. *Steve Patterson*

CHAPTER TWO

REACHING THE PACIFIC

The Chicago, Milwaukee & St. Paul Railway of 1890 was a transportation entity of considerable importance in the region it served. It generated $26.4 million in revenues in the fiscal year ending June 30, 1890, equivalent to $4,668 per mile. In that year, it carried 9.2 million tons of freight and more than 7.5 million passengers. On an average day its trains ran more than 53,000 miles.

The CM&StP's route map remained relatively unchanged during the 1890s. The one exception involved an acquisition early in the

Acquisition of the Milwaukee & Northern in 1890 gave the CM&StP access to Green Bay and the iron-mining region of Michigan's Upper Peninsula. Here, a northbound freight from Milwaukee crosses the Fox River at Green Bay in December 1984. *Steve Glischinski*

decade: the Milwaukee & Northern Railroad Company, which gave the CM&StP a presence in the iron-mining region on the Upper Peninsula of Michigan. The M&N came under control of the CM&StP in September 1890, and was absorbed into the parent company in June 1893.

Even though it was taking a breather after the rapid expansion of the 1880s, the CM&StP could not stand idle. Track had to be upgraded to handle heavier tonnages. Iron rails were replaced with steel, and wooden bridges gave way to iron structures. Equipment was modernized with automatic couplers, air brakes, and, on passenger cars, steam heat. The railroad invested in shops, roundhouses, turntables, yards, freight houses, and signal systems. Where traffic was heaviest, the right-of-way was reballasted, widened, and regraded, and in some places second main tracks were added.

The CM&StP was not alone in shifting its focus from geographic expansion to improving what it already had. In fact, the national rail system had become overextended. In the late 1880s, construction of new rail lines fell off dramatically. The rapid growth of the rail network had been one element in the country's economic prosperity, since it created both employment and the demand for raw materials. The curtailment of railway construction coincided with a decline in the agricultural economy, brought on by drought and overproduction. By early 1893 the country found itself in an economic depression—the Panic of 1893. Some weaker railroads, including Northern Pacific and Union Pacific, began to fail.

In the same year, an event occurred that would be of lasting importance to the country in general and to the railroad industry in particular: the founding of the American Railway Union by Eugene V. Debs.

The CM&StP considered itself an enlightened employer. Nevertheless, in 1894 it found itself, like every other railroad west of Chicago, affected by a general strike called by Debs in response to actions of the Pullman Company. One irony, as far as the CM&StP was concerned, was that it had canceled its contract with Pullman for the operation of sleeping cars a few years earlier, but that fact did not give it immunity in the eyes of the strikers.

The loss of revenue resulting from the strike (amounting to $500,000 in July 1894, according to Derleth) only aggravated the effects of the depression that had started the previous year. The strike and the depression, serious as they were, were both transitory events, and by 1896 the CM&StP was back on solid financial footing. However, the Debs strike marked the end of the "management knows best" era of labor relations at the CM&StP and every other major railroad.

This map portrays the scope of the CM&StP's network in 1888. Still in the future: acquisition of the Milwaukee & Northern to Green Bay and Iron Mountain in 1893; completion of the line from Chamberlain to Rapid City in 1907; opening of the Puget Sound extension in 1909; and extension to Indiana in 1921. *Milwaukee Road Archives of the Milwaukee Public Library*

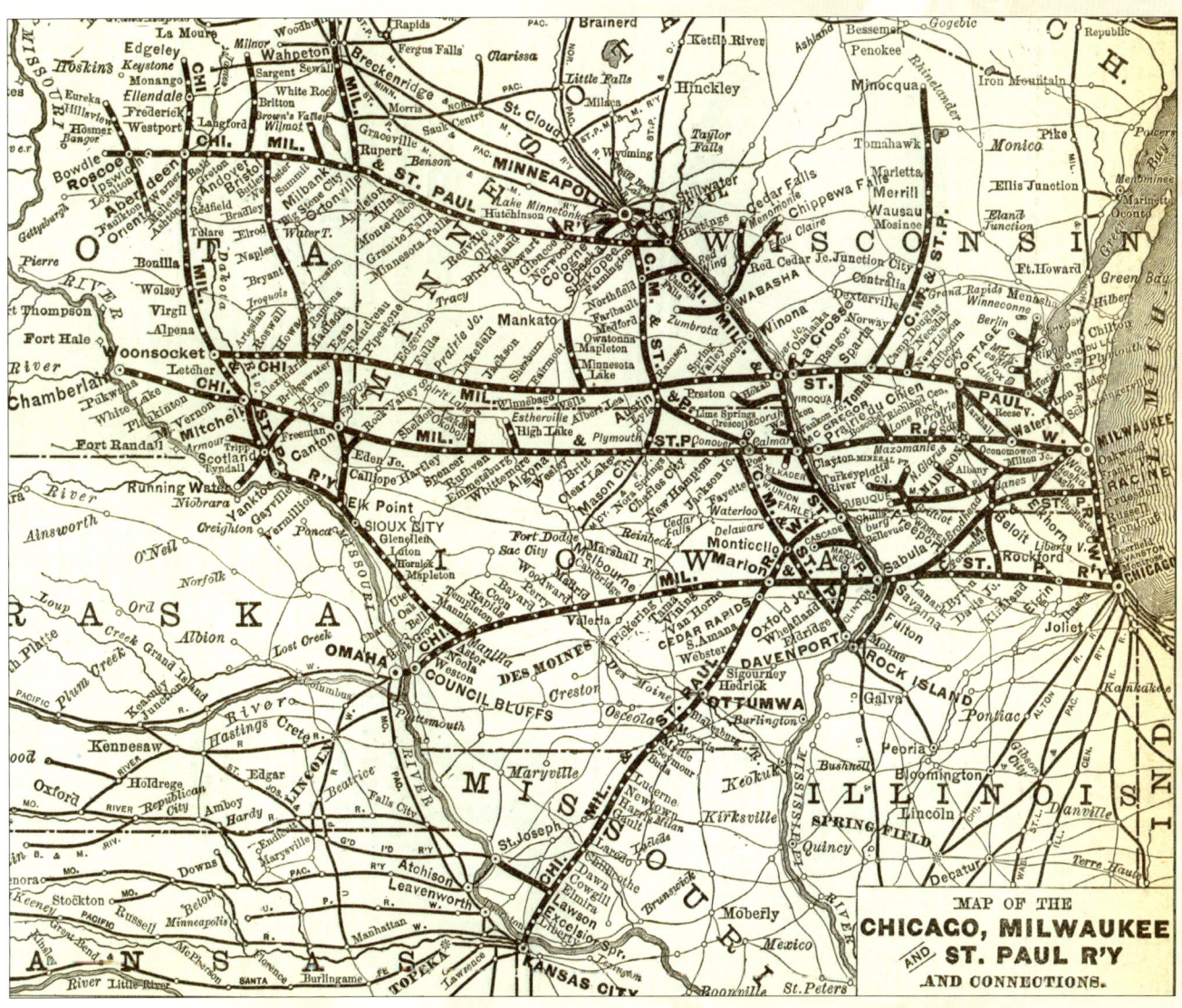

Right: In a CM&StP promotional booklet for the Puget Sound Line, the bridge across the Missouri River at Mobridge, South Dakota, is described as follows: "Three towering spans, each 425 feet in length, rising sixty-five feet above the rails, and four massive piers, that lift the superstructure fifty-five feet above the stream, distinguish this as the heaviest bridge ever thrown across the great river." *Author collection*

Bottom: A profile of the line between Tacoma, Washington, and Miles City, Montana, from the Milwaukee's 1946 annual report. *Author collection*

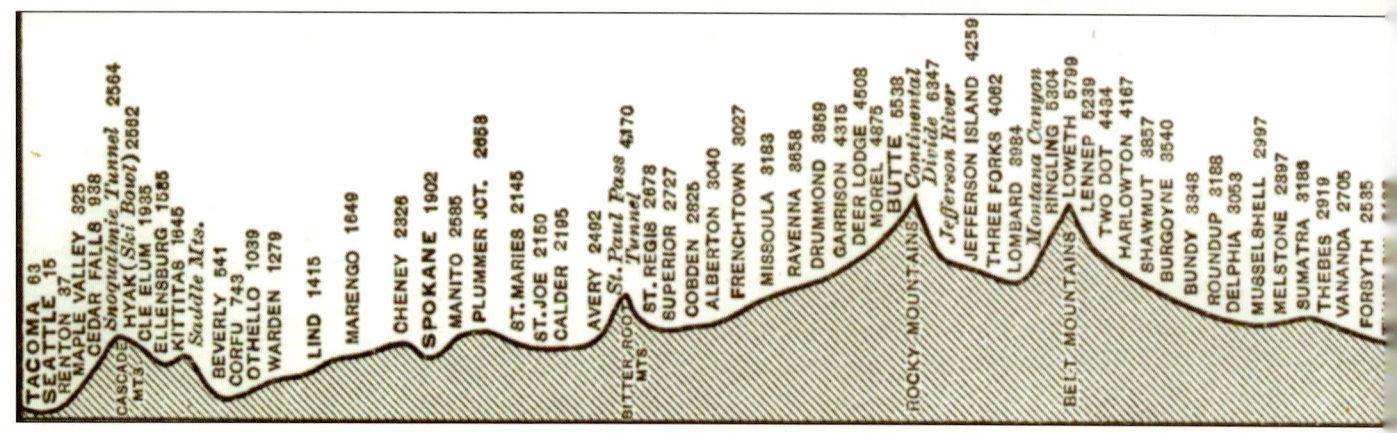

The emergence of organized labor was not the only external force that would affect the CM&StP's ability to chart its own course. Capitalists were organizing, too. Industrialists who built their fortunes in oil, meatpacking, banking, and other businesses joined forces as necessary to pursue common interests, and in many cases found themselves seated next to one another in railroad boardrooms. Many of the familiar names in the pantheon of late-nineteenth-century business giants would influence the CM&StP either as members of its board of directors (William Rockefeller and Philip Armour) or as participants in the struggle for control of the midwestern rail network (James J. Hill, J. P. Morgan, and E. H. Harriman).

As W. H. Schmidt, Jr., summarized the company's situation in the journal *Railroad History* (Issue No. 136, Spring 1977), "the Milwaukee remained jealous of its independence and fought against being drawn into

The Milwaukee's bridge across the Columbia River at Beverly, Washington, was an imposing structure in a majestic setting. Here, a westbound freight prepares to climb Boylston Hill out of the river valley in July 1979. *Steve Glischinski*

mastery by eastern financial powers." But as a result of its geographic position, "the Milwaukee, reluctantly, was drawn into a nationwide struggle between industrial giants."

Why Go West?

The CM&StP got a new president in 1899: Albert J. Earling, who was 50 years old and had risen through the operating department since joining the company in 1866. Earling would preside over vast changes at the railroad.

However, from 1900 to the end of The Milwaukee Road's existence 85 years later, James J. Hill, who never owned a share of stock in the railroad or served in its management, had a bigger influence on the company than any of its owners or managers. He had built the Great Northern Railway from St. Paul west, reaching Seattle in 1893. In 1896, he acquired control of GN rival Northern Pacific (NP), which had completed its line between St. Paul and Puget Sound in 1883.

Hill's banker was J. P. Morgan, who in the 1890s had helped refinance (and then became a director of) several eastern railroads. Hill and Morgan recognized that to strengthen their hold on rail traffic to and from the Pacific Northwest, they needed a route between St. Paul and Chicago. Clearly, the CM&StP would have served this purpose. But Hill and Morgan were rebuffed

The Chicago, Milwaukee & Puget Sound was the CM&StP subsidiary that encompassed the lines from Mobridge, South Dakota, west, until being absorbed by the parent company at the end of 1912. This is the inside cover of a promotional booklet issued in 1911. *Author collection*

Five General Electric "Bi-Polar" locomotives were built in 1919 and 1920, and soon became the symbol of the CM&StP's electrified operations. As Noel T. Holley describes them in his book, *The Milwaukee Electrics*, "they caught the fancy of America. They came to symbolize the Milwaukee Road and the *Olympian*, a train called 'The Best to the East . . .' The Bi-Polars had a distinct kind of beauty, and this, coupled with their other attributes, made them good for public relations." This advertisement is from 1925. *Author collection*

when they made overtures to the company's principal shareholders regarding a possible lease of the CM&StP.

In 1900, Hill and Morgan achieved their objective of a St. Paul–Chicago route when an opportunity developed for them to gain control of the Chicago, Burlington & Quincy (CB&Q). This deal, Derleth writes, "drew the lines for continuing battle between the railroad giants of the midwest."

As a vehicle for their ownership of CB&Q and NP stock, Hill and Morgan created the Northern Securities Corporation in 1901. E. H. Harriman, who controlled the Union Pacific Railroad and who had contested the Hill-Morgan interests for control of CB&Q and NP, was given a place on the Northern Securities board of directors, as was William Rockefeller. In 1904, the trust-busting efforts of Theodore Roosevelt resulted in the dissolution of Northern Securities. However, Hill and Morgan remained in control of both Great Northern and Northern Pacific, and those two carriers in turn shared control of CB&Q.

The CM&StP faced a dilemma. On the one hand, the nature of U.S. rail traffic was changing, with longer hauls across regional boundaries becoming more common, and with the ever-increasing importance of international trade. On the other hand, the CM&StP was now surrounded by carriers whose reach was greater than its own. The Hill lines were only the most obvious case. Several railroads competed for traffic between

Above: In the mid-1920s, CM&StP issued a promotional booklet titled "Lake Michigan to Puget Sound: A Scenic Guide Book," containing 21 prints of hand-colored photos. Most of the photos accentuate the line's scenic wonders, with one exception: "King of the Rails" Bi-Polar 10252. Built in 1918, this locomotive was renumbered E3 in 1939, and retired in 1961. *Author collection*

Right: One of the original boxcab motors waits for a helper assignment up the hill out of Avery, Idaho, in the early 1960s. *Don Sims*

At the substations in electrified territory, AC power was converted to DC, which was then transmitted to the distribution system where the locomotives' pantographs drew power from the trolley wire. This substation, at East Portal, Montana, was the largest such structure on the Milwaukee's electrified territory. *Phil Mason*

Chicago and Omaha, for interchange with Union Pacific, but Illinois Central and Chicago & North Western both had friendlier relationships with UP than did the CM&StP. Another Upper Midwest carrier, the Minneapolis, St. Paul & Sault Ste. Marie (Soo Line), was under the control of Canadian Pacific; the Soo's gateway with CP at Portal, North Dakota, allowed it to send traffic to the West Coast.

Every railroad that connected the Upper Midwest to the Pacific already had an alliance of some kind in the CM&StP's home territory. This would put the CM&StP at a disadvantage in negotiating rates and divisions. In the minds of the CM&StP's managers and owners, there was but one course of action open to them: to build a line of their own to the West Coast.

The one threat that might have deterred them, if they had had perfect foreknowledge of what would happen in the coming decade, was the building of the Panama Canal. However, this possibility was dismissed as unlikely, given the political, engineering, and other obstacles that stood in its way. If it did come to pass, the conventional wisdom (or at least the perception of the CM&StP's directors) was that the canal would be a conduit for military traffic only, not for commercial freight.

The idea of building west percolated for a time, and on November 28, 1905, the board of directors of the Chicago, Milwaukee and St. Paul Railway authorized the construction of a line of railroad to Puget Sound. Five months earlier, John F. Stevens had been hired as the chief engineer of the Panama Canal. It was a milestone to which the CM&StP's board of directors might have paid more heed, although they were not alone in viewing the canal as a boondoggle that would never be built.

Construction on the Puget Sound extension started in April 1906. From a point in South Dakota just east of the Missouri River, the line would go northwest, cut across the southwest corner of North Dakota, and then cross Montana, through Miles City and Butte. From Butte, the line would run northwest to Missoula, and across northern Idaho into Washington. It would cross the Cascade Mountains at Snoqualmie Pass and thence into Seattle and Tacoma. The Milwaukee's Chicago–St. Paul–Seattle route would be 130 miles shorter than CB&Q–NP, and 22 miles shorter than CB&Q–GN.

When the board had approved the extension, they were working with a construction cost estimate of $60 million. But the engineering standards to which the line was built, plus the speed of construction (three years, almost to the day) and the unforeseen challenges of pushing a railroad through remote, unpopulated territory, increased the actual cost of construction. By 1926, following the electrification, a total of $250 million had been invested in the line. As Carlos A. Schwantes summed it up in his book, *Railroad Signatures Across the Pacific Northwest*, "that princely sum purchased a well-engineered right-of-way that crossed five mountain ranges and served a country as rich in scenery as it was devoid of population centers."

From east to west, the new line crossed the Belt Mountains, the Rockies, the Bitter Root range, the Saddle Mountains, and the Cascades. The line included 45 tunnels. The longest, at St. Paul Pass, was 8,771 feet in length. Grades over Snoqualmie Pass were reduced through a project that included the building of an 11,890-foot tunnel, which opened in January 1915.

More than 55 years after its December 1916 construction date, Milwaukee boxcab E29A is still in service, as part of the Butte helper, in October 1972. *Tom Murray*

Building across these mountain ranges, challenging as it was, was not the only obstacle to be surmounted by construction crews. Even in the relatively flat territory across South Dakota and eastern Montana, crews found that the absence of roads and the difficulties of access increased the cost of building the railroad.

In eastern Montana, the line followed the Yellowstone River. The Northern Pacific already occupied one bank of the river, leaving the opposite bank available to the CM&StP, but crews found, as Derleth describes it, that "all grading outfits, teams, steam shovels, and so forth had to be conveyed across [the river] at considerable expense and trouble. . . . Large portions of the road had to be protected by wing dams against the Yellowstone's predatory rises," since otherwise "high water always caused considerable damage and the loss of thousands of yards of material."

On its way west, the CM&StP encountered two existing railroads that helped it reach its destination sooner than it would have otherwise. The first was the Montana Railroad (also known as the "Jawbone line"), which occupied a strategic position in central Montana. The railroad had been started in 1893, running from a connection with the Northern Pacific at Lombard, eastward toward a silver deposit in the Castle Mountains. It crossed the Big Belt Mountains, the easternmost of the mountain ranges that the CM&StP had to contend with. The CM&StP leased and then purchased the railroad and, though it had to be completely rebuilt, it solved a significant routing problem for the builders of the Puget Sound extension.

The second railroad that assisted the CM&StP's westward progress was the Butte, Anaconda & Pacific, a subsidiary of Anaconda Copper Mining Company. Until the CM&StP could complete its own line west of Butte through Silver Bow Canyon in 1913, the BA&P extended trackage rights to CM&StP trains.

The last spike ceremony on the Puget Sound route was held at a point 4 miles west

of Garrison, Montana, on May 19, 1909, and the line opened for business on July 4, 1909. Schwantes notes that "For the next two years it provided service during daylight hours only . . . because of the newness of the roadbed and the volume of construction still in progress." In May 1911, through passenger service between Chicago and Seattle was inaugurated with the *Olympian* and *Columbian*.

The CM&StP issued postcards, brochures, and other promotional material to tout the scenery on its new western route. This postcard shows the *Olympian* descending the eastern slope of the Rockies, with boxcab 10100AB leading. The 12 passenger-service boxcabs were relegated to freight service within four years of delivery, following the arrival of passenger locomotives from General Electric and Westinghouse. *Author collection*

Milwaukee Extra 24 East at Plummer, Idaho, in August 1977. The line diverging to the right goes to Spokane and Metaline Falls, Washington. *Steve Patterson*

The original western terminus of the western extension was Tacoma. Why Tacoma, rather than Seattle? In their book, *Milwaukee Road West*, Charles R. Wood and Dorothy M. Wood offer several reasons: it was located "in the heart of the western Washington lumbering area, from which the Milwaukee planned to derive its greatest single source of traffic"; it "offered one of the best harbors on the entire Pacific Coast"; the dominance of the port of Seattle by GN and NP would make it difficult for CM&StP to secure facilities there; and the city of Tacoma was willing to offer the CM&StP "a favorable economic and political climate." The CM&StP did reach Seattle on trackage rights from the mainline at Black River Junction, a distance of 9 miles, but Tacoma remained the operational anchor of the western extension for the next seven decades.

Traffic on the mainline alone would not be enough to justify the cost of construction,

Next page: In Washington, the Milwaukee had an extensive network of branchlines to serve the forest products industry, as shown in this 1928 map. *Author collection*

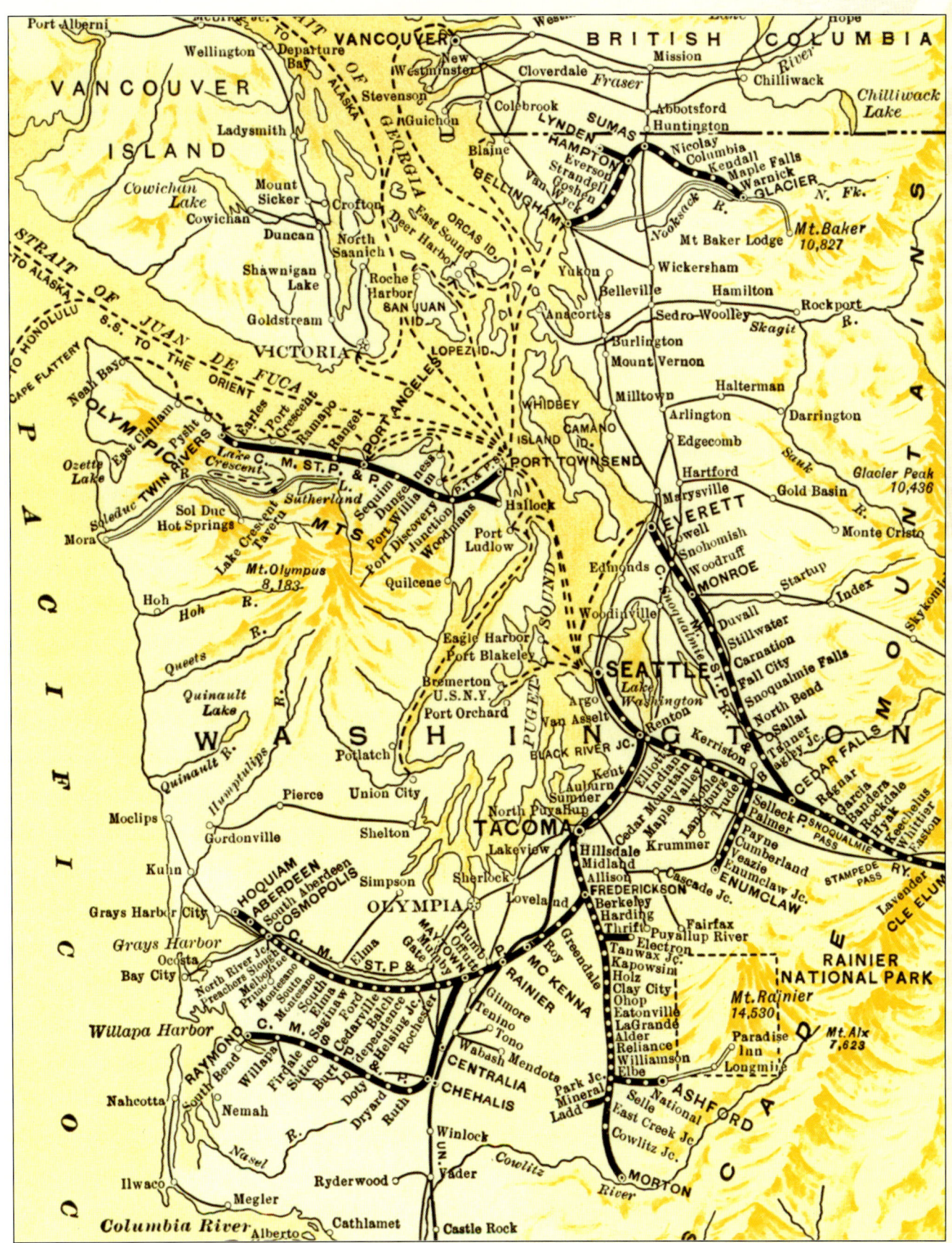

so between 1909 and 1917 the CM&StP built and purchased several hundred miles of branches in South Dakota, North Dakota, Montana, Idaho, and Washington to feed traffic to and from the Pacific extension. One important addition to the route was a line from Plummer Junction, Idaho, to Marengo, Washington, via Spokane, which was bypassed by the original route. The Spokane Line, required primarily for passenger trains, opened in 1914 using a combination of new construction and trackage rights over UP's Oregon-Washington Railroad & Navigation Company subsidiary.

Electrification

The CM&StP's route might be better-engineered and shorter than either of the Hill lines, but that was not enough of a distinction for the company's management. Even before the line was completed, the CM&StP began to examine the merits of electrifying the route through the mountains. The economic argument for electrification was based on several factors, including the low cost of hydroelectric power in the Pacific Northwest. In addition, steam locomotives were high-maintenance machines, requiring coal, water, and cleaning at frequent intervals. They were not well suited to overcome the extremes of low winter temperatures and steep ascending grades on the new line. Electrification would also eliminate the threat of crews being asphyxiated by smoke in the line's many tunnels.

Regenerative braking was another plus. It allowed an electric locomotive descending a grade to turn its traction motors into generators; instead of taking electricity from the overhead wires, the train would put electricity into the system. It also made trains easier to control on descending grades.

Regardless of electrification's merits, the CM&StP's board of directors also had as one of its members an advocate who may have

been less than objective: John D. Ryan, founder of Montana Power Company and president of Anaconda Copper. Ryan became a director of the CM&StP in 1909. Schwantes notes that Anaconda ultimately sold 12,000 tons of copper to the railroad.

The yard at Harlowton, Montana, at the eastern end of the Rocky Mountain Division electrified territory, shows why linemen were as important as trackmen in keeping the railroad operating. *Steve Patterson*

The decision to electrify was supported by early results of the smaller-scale electrification of Anaconda Copper's Butte, Anaconda & Pacific (BA&P), which went into service in 1913. In his book, *When the Steam Railroads Electrified*, William D. Middleton describes a 1914 economic assessment of the BA&P electrification. It found that, in comparison with steam operations, electric locomotives allowed an 8.8 percent increase in gross ton-miles with 26 percent fewer trains and "an overall savings of more than 36 percent."

The CM&StP selected a system similar to the BA&P's 2,400-volt direct current overhead-wire technology, except that the CM&StP upped the voltage on its system to 3,000. Substations to convert 100,000-volt alternating current power (purchased from Ryan's Montana Power Company) to DC were located at average intervals of 32 miles.

The CM&StP electrification was initially done in two segments: from Harlowton, Montana, to Avery, Idaho (438 miles, opened in November 1916); and from Othello, Washington, to Tacoma (207 miles, opened in March 1920). The last 9-mile section from Black River Junction, Washington, to Seattle opened in July 1927. When it was completed, the railroad had 656 miles under wire—a number that appeared on the cover of the Milwaukee's public timetables for several years.

Locomotives were supplied by a partnership between American Locomotive Company and General Electric Company. Middleton describes the 42 two-unit boxcab units initially purchased: "Thirty locomotives intended for freight service were geared for a maximum speed of 30 mph. The remaining 12, intended for passenger operation, were identical except for 60-mph gearing, oil-fired train-heating boilers, and train-lighting panels."

The boxcabs, built in 1915 and 1916, were augmented by two 70-ton GE steeplecab switchers built in 1916 (and two similar 82-ton units constructed in 1919); five Bi-Polar GE passenger locomotives for passenger operations on the Washington electrified zone, built in 1918 and 1919; and ten Baldwin-Westinghouse passenger locomotives for the Montana-Idaho zone, delivered in 1919 and 1920. With the delivery of the passenger locomotives, the 12 boxcabs originally assigned to passenger service were reassigned to freight.

The railroad got every ounce of publicity that it could from this technological marvel. It was the longest rail electrification project in North America, and traversed by far the most rugged territory. The cleanliness of electrified operations gave the railroad a good reason for suggesting to passengers that, in choosing which railroad to patronize, they should consider what type of locomotive was pulling their train, and not just conventional amenities like sleeping car and dining service.

The Cost of Becoming a Transcontinental Railroad

The construction of a line to the Pacific Northwest was made possible in part by the robust financial condition that the CM&StP enjoyed during the first years of the twentieth century. The operating ratio (the ratio of operating expenses, excluding taxes and additions to property, to revenues) was 60.2 percent, a very favorable number. Funded debt stood at $122 million. CM&StP earned three times its fixed charges (consisting of interest on the company's bonds), indicating that it was resilient enough to withstand an economic downturn or other adversity without jeopardizing its payments to debt holders.

Construction was carried out by separate companies incorporated in each of the five states traversed by the new line, but eventually these entities were combined into a single subsidiary, the Chicago, Milwaukee & Puget Sound Railway. On December 24, 1912, that subsidiary was absorbed by the parent company.

Addition of the western lines to the company increased the length of main track owned solely by CM&StP by 2,159 miles, to 9,425 miles, as of June 30, 1913, an increase of almost 30 percent. Including jointly owned lines and trackage used under contracts, the company operated 9,613 route miles as of mid-1913.

Earling was succeeded as president by Harry E. Byram in October 1917. By that time, the environment in which CM&StP operated had begun to change. The Panama Canal had been open for three years. The cost of fuel, labor, and other resources was on the increase.

At the end of 1917, the Milwaukee was operating 10,257 route miles, and the first phase of the electrification had been completed. Financially, however, the company was not as healthy as it had been in 1905, in part because the cost of the extension was much greater than the estimate of $60 million relied upon by the board of directors in 1905. Derleth gives the actual cost as "$256,968,126, inclusive of $22,990,254 for electrification." Other sources note that this figure includes post-construction costs that ought to have been charged to operating expenses rather than to the capital expenditure account.

Whatever the true cost of the western extension, its construction coincided with an increase of $368 million in the company's debt over the period from 1905 to 1917. In the latter year, funded debt stood at $490 million. The operating ratio had increased to 75.4 percent—not a bad number, but trending in the wrong direction. The company earned only about 1.2 times its fixed charges, a much slimmer margin of safety than it had enjoyed in 1905. While CM&StP could be a viable enterprise based on its revenues and expenses, the debt load would be a challenge in the years to come.

Aside from costing more than expected, the traffic-generating capacity of the western extension was also constrained by the fact that most existing rail shippers in the region were already served by either GN or NP. These railroads required the CM&StP to interchange traffic moving to and from such customers at St. Paul, denying the Milwaukee its long haul and undermining the economic rationale for the Puget Sound extension.

In short, by making the decision to build to Puget Sound, the CM&StP's board of directors had made a bet. No one could know as of 1917 how that wager would turn out, but it was becoming clear that it was a much larger bet than anyone had realized in 1905.

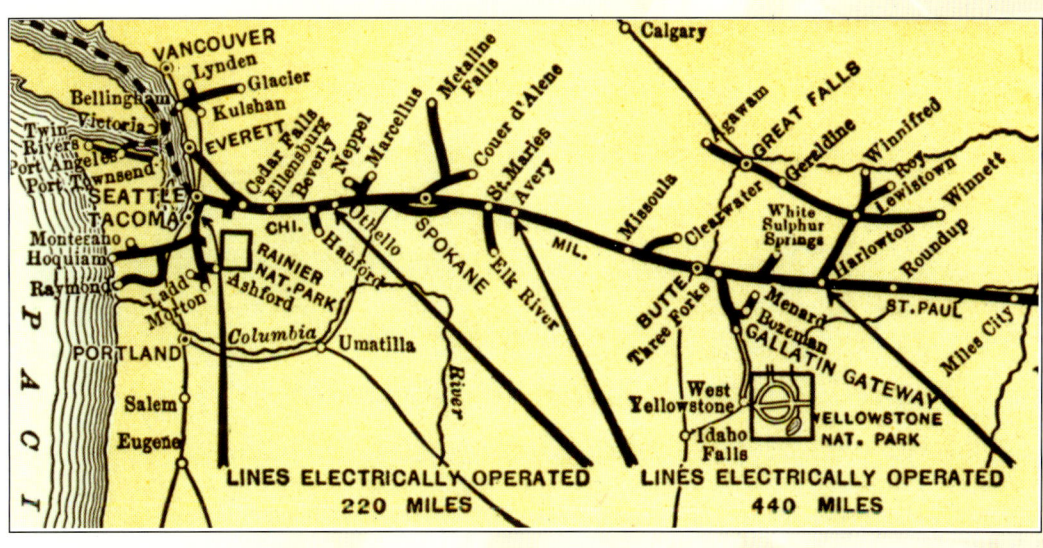

A 1928 map of the Milwaukee's routes west of Miles City, Montana. *Author collection*

Sayner, Wisconsin, was at milepost 177.5 of the Wisconsin Valley Line from New Lisbon to Star Lake. In the early 1920s a mixed train ran three days a week between Minocqua (MP 164.4) and the end of the line at Star Lake (MP 183.3). This photo was taken around 1922. *Wisconsin Historical Society/Image WHi-24652*

CHAPTER THREE

BETWEEN TWO WORLD WARS

In December 1917, the government began its takeover of the nation's railroads in an effort to improve their efficiency and responsiveness to the needs of World War I. From the CM&StP's perspective, the federal takeover of the nation's railroads could hardly have come at a worse time. Having taken on hundreds of millions of dollars in debt in order to transform itself from a regional carrier to a transcontinental, the CM&StP needed to focus on putting traffic on the new routes and on making the enlarged railroad function as a unified and efficient

After a train set out cars at a station, the waybills were left behind so that an agent, operator, or clerk could prepare a switch list to ensure that cars got to their assigned destinations. Here, the conductor of an eastbound train hands off a packet of waybills at Green Island, Iowa, in February 1978. *Joe McMillan*

network. It could ill afford to lose control of its operations and finances. Yet that was exactly what happened during the two-plus years of operation under the U.S. Railroad Administration (USRA), from late 1917 to early 1920.

When the government assumed control of the railroad in December 1917, it seized the company's cash and accounts receivable. In its annual report for 1918, CM&StP management said this left it "with no funds to meet current expenses and other corporate requirements." It was, therefore, forced to borrow to meet its day-to-day needs.

Despite assurances that the nation's railroads would be returned to their owners in substantially the same condition as when they were placed under government control, the USRA period took a significant physical toll on the CM&StP. As August Derleth states in his history of the company, by early 1920, "the company's rolling stock was sadly depleted and depreciated."

The operating ratio, which had begun to climb even prior to federal control, rose to 92 percent in both 1918 and 1919, and even higher—to an unsustainable 98 percent—in 1920, when the company was returned to private operation.

Eastward to Indiana

Despite (or perhaps because of) the financial pressures it faced, CM&StP's management in the early 1920s focused on improving the road's efficiency. One important element in the company's cost structure was fuel for its locomotives. With no significant online coal reserves, Byram went searching for a solution. He found it in the Chicago, Terre Haute and Southeastern (CTH&SE), a 373-mile railroad that ran south from a connection with the Baltimore & Ohio Chicago Terminal Company at Chicago Heights, Illinois. It then crossed into Indiana and passed through coalfields in the vicinity of Terre Haute.

The CM&StP leased the CTH&SE in June 1921. In January 1922 it entered into a related transaction, acquiring control of the Chicago, Milwaukee & Gary Railway. The CM&G was a belt line around Chicago (using trackage rights over the Elgin, Joliet & Eastern for part of its route) that gave the

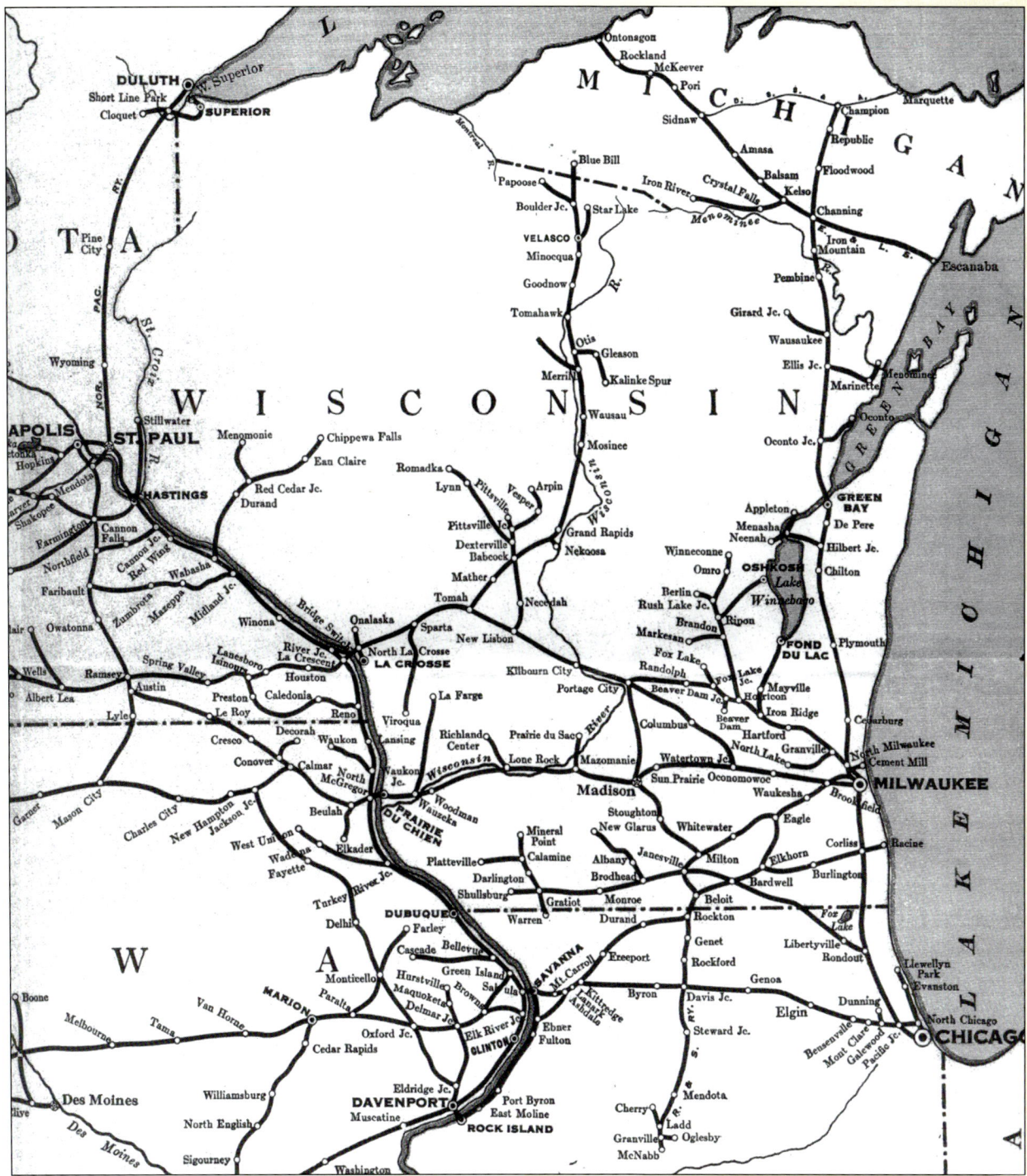

A 1915 map.
Author collection

CM&StP access to the CTH&SE without having to use other railroads' trackage through the congested Chicago terminal.

The extension of the CM&StP into Indiana gave it a distinction not shared by any other western railroad: it was the only such railroad to extend east of the Chicago gateway. However, the Indiana route would not become a significant traffic generator until after the Milwaukee gained access to Louisville in 1973.

Whatever benefits these two railroads may have had in terms of assuring the

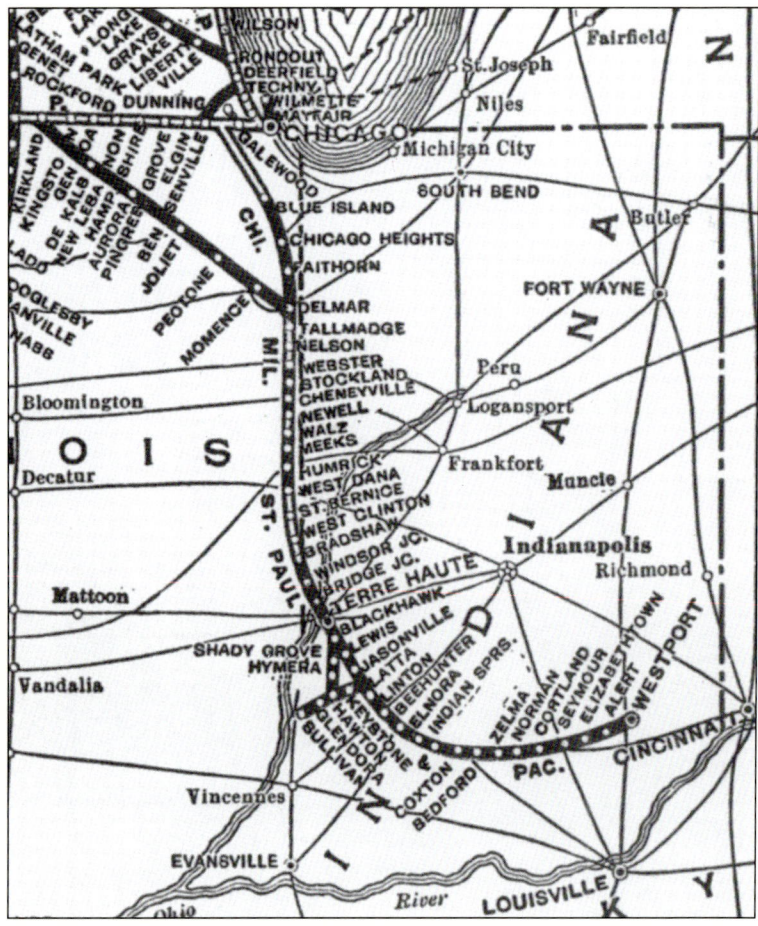

Detail from a 1940 Milwaukee Road map shows the company's lines between the Chicago area and southern Indiana. *Author collection*

CM&StP an adequate supply of coal, they only added to the company's debt load. The 999-year lease of the CTH&SE included a guarantee that the CM&StP would pay interest on that company's $22 million in bonds. The CM&G deal brought with it a guarantee to pay off $3 million in bonds.

Despite its disappointing financial results, the CM&StP was able to make some improvements to equipment in the early 1920s. In 1920, 100 2-8-2 Mikado-type locomotives, ordered by USRA, arrived, as did 4,000 boxcars, and an additional 100 Mikados were ordered for delivery in 1920 and 1921. In 1921, the company ordered 2,500 gondola cars. The following year, orders were placed for 3,500 boxcars and 500 automobile cars.

In the period from 1920 to 1924, the railroad increased the size of its equipment roster by 288 steam locomotives and 2,421 freight cars, excluding those acquired from the CTH&SE. The new equipment was more modern, with greater hauling capacity. The average number of cars on the road's freight trains rose from 35.7 in 1921 to 40.7 in 1924, and average tons of freight per train rose from 562 to 680 over the same period.

Bankruptcy

While some of CM&StP's problems were of its own making, in other respects it was a victim of forces beyond its control. The ability of CM&StP and every other U.S. railroad to set prices for their services was constrained by the Interstate Commerce Commission, a situation that would not change in any meaningful way until 1980. The ICC was a political body whose constituency was the shipping public, not the railroads or their investors. Reductions in freight rates in January and July 1922 cost the company millions in revenues. From 1921 to 1924, average revenue per ton declined by 18 percent, from $3.08 to $2.54.

And regardless of whether the CM&StP's board of directors should have anticipated the building of the Panama Canal when they authorized the Puget Sound extension in 1905, the company's executives and managers in the decades that followed had to deal with the canal as a *fait accompli*. It was the source of much hand-wringing by management over the years, such as this statement in the annual report for 1923: "Your company did not enjoy the same prosperity as railroads in some other sections of the country on account of unfavorable business conditions in some parts of the territory it serves, and also on account of its inability to make rates to the Pacific Coast to meet water competition through the Panama Canal."

The company's operating results for 1923 showed great improvement since the dismal year of 1920. For the first time since 1917, the operating ratio was below 80, at

Above: The Milwaukee Road's train from Louisville to Bensenville, Illinois, uses Louisville & Nashville (former Monon) trackage rights at New Albany, Indiana, across the Ohio River from Louisville, in October 1975. The train is powered by two GP20s bracketing a GP9. *Bob Anderson* Right: Latta, 24 miles south of Terre Haute, was the Milwaukee's principal terminal in southern Indiana. A Milwaukee GP20 is coupled to an Illinois Central Geep at Latta in April 1979. The Milwaukee interchanged with IC at Linton, 8 miles to the south. *Dave Gayer*

79.6 percent. Railway operating income amounted to $26 million. Yet, after deducting equipment and other rents, as well as interest payments of more than $20 million, the company was left with net income of only $207,686—barely breakeven.

The annual report for 1924 was prefaced with this brief paragraph:

"On March 18th, 1925, by order of the District Court of the United States for the Northern District of Illinois, Eastern Division, H. E. Byram, Mark W. Potter and Edward J. Brundage were appointed Receivers of the property and franchises of the Chicago, Milwaukee & St. Paul Railway Company."

The bottom line had turned negative in 1924, with a net deficit of $1.9 million. Again operating performance was adequate,

Top: In harsh winters, locomotive walkways would often fill up with snow, as they have on the lead GP38-2 of this westbound train at Monroe Center, Illinois, in February 1982. *John Leopard* Above: The 45-mile Davenport, Rock Island & North Western Railway, commonly known as the "DRI-Line," was a switching and terminal company in the Quad Cities. From 1901 to 1995, ownership was evenly split between the Chicago, Burlington & Quincy and Milwaukee Road and their successors. In July 1981, a DRI&NW transfer from Bettendorf to East Moline crosses the Mississippi River on the Crescent Bridge, which was placed into service in 1900. *John Leopard*

with an operating ratio almost the same as 1923's, but interest on debt was $700,000 greater than the previous year. Total funded debt was more than $594 million—an increase of $104 million since 1917. The company's operating cash flow was simply inadequate to support this level of debt.

Of The Milwaukee Road's three bankruptcies in the twentieth century, the one that began in March 1925 was the shortest and least painful. In contrast to almost any corporate bankruptcy that might occur today, shareholders emerged with something to show for their investment. The bankruptcy served its intended purpose of giving the company a temporary breather from the burdensome interest payments required by its huge debt load.

Derleth reports, "the receivers directed that all the fixed property of the road not in acceptable shape should be repaired without delay." Investments were also made in rolling stock. Equipment used on major passenger trains was equipped with roller bearings. This made the cars easier to pull, and virtually eliminated the potential for overheated bearings, commonly known as "hotboxes."

A "New" Milwaukee Road

There was only a single reorganization plan, put forward by bankers Kuhn, Loeb & Company and National City Bank. In March 1927, a new company, Chicago, Milwaukee, St. Paul and Pacific Railroad Company, was organized, and it took over the property on January 13, 1928. In its first annual report, the new company showed 10,107 route-miles owned solely by the company and a total of 11,252 route-miles in operation. The three states with the greatest Milwaukee Road mileage were Iowa (1,861 miles), South Dakota (1,796), and Wisconsin (1,747).

Additions to the equipment fleet during 1928 were valued at $8.4 million and included 1,600 boxcars, 650 stock cars, 552 coal cars,

A CM&StP timetable from December 1922 shows 649 miles of electrification. The number was updated to 656 following completion of the electrification to Seattle in 1927. *Author collection*

53

Grand Crossing at North La Crosse, Wisconsin, was originally the site where four railroads crossed: the Milwaukee; Burlington; North Western; and a Green Bay & Western predecessor. The GB&W was gone by the time this tower was constructed in the late 1920s, but the crossing remained complex, requiring many levers to control its switches and signals, as shown here in February 1978. The tower remained in service until 1991, and has been preserved at Copeland Park in La Crosse. *Photo by Philip Hastings, courtesy of California State Railroad Museum/negative no. 3136*

and 300 automobile cars, as well as 164 gondolas converted to flatcars. The railroad had installed automatic train control between Portage and La Crosse and Centralized Traffic Control between Tunnel City and Raymore, all on the La Crosse Division. Grade separation work in Chicago, which had been underway for several years, continued, as did similar projects in Milwaukee and in Evanston, Illinois. Modern rail ranging in weight from 90 to 130 pounds per yard replaced older, lighter rail, with 61,847 tons of new rail installed in 1923.

Byram, after serving as both president and receiver, had been elevated to chairman of the board, and Henry A. Scandrett had arrived from Union Pacific to take over as president. Results for the first year of operation (minus the first 13 days of January, prior to acquisition of the property by the new company) showed net income of $9.3 million.

Despite having been given a fresh start as a result of the bankruptcy, the new management did not strike an optimistic tone in its first report to shareholders: "While the 1928 results are very substantially better than those of any previous year since the beginning of Federal control, and so afford ground for encouragement, they still fall far short of what they should be." Return on investment, the company said, was either 3.84 percent or 4.17 percent, depending on whose valuation figures were used (management's or the ICC's), but in either case fell short of what the ICC considered a fair rate of return, 5.75 percent. The company laid much of the blame on the "whittling process"—the cumulative effect of rate reductions ordered by the ICC.

The capital structure of the new Milwaukee gave it very little maneuverability, as would become evident in the coming years. It was still highly leveraged, with $459 million in funded debt versus $257 million in shareholders' equity.

The report for 1928 was written in early 1929, well before October's stock market crash. Even in early 1930, when the 1929 report was produced (showing net income of $7.0 million, a 24 percent drop versus the prior year), there seemed to be no sense of alarm about the overall economic situation.

However, financial results for 1930 *were* alarming. Milwaukee management told its shareholders that "the world-wide industrial depression" had "reduced sharply the volume of business and revenues of your company." Revenues dropped 20 percent from the 1929 level. After making $22.8 million in interest payments on bonds and other debt, the Milwaukee was left with a deficit of $4.9 million.

Milwaukee caboose 992074, at the rear of an eastbound train, passes the tower at Newport, Minnesota, in July 1973. In an article in *The Milwaukee Railroader*, Steve Glischinski described the operating arrangement on this 16-mile section of the railroad: "Between St. Croix Tower and St. Paul, the CB&Q and CMStP&P . . . established joint track that essentially created a double-track main line for the two roads . . . controlled by a dispatcher in the tower at Newport." *Tom Murray*

The situation got worse in 1931, as the Depression deepened and a drought in Minnesota, the Dakotas, and Montana combined to drag down revenues a full 35 percent from their 1929 levels. The following year, 1932, revenues were less than half what they had been in 1929.

Over the period from 1929 to 1932, the company's management was able to bring down operating expenses almost in lockstep with revenues, a significant achievement given the fact that expenses don't automatically go away when traffic slumps. Many hard decisions were required to decide where maintenance dollars should go; rail and tie programs were among the victims of the cutbacks.

The slide in revenues finally stopped in 1933, when they came in at $85.5 million, roughly $600,000 ahead of 1932 levels. Revenues improved again in 1934, but they were still down 48.7 percent since 1929.

Passenger traffic was particularly hard hit during this period. In 1929, The Milwaukee Road carried 7.4 million passengers; in 1934 only 3.2 million passengers used the railroad. However, passenger service could not be cut in proportion to the decline in business. On average, in 1934 the company operated 3.15 passenger trains per day on each mile of the railroad, down from 4.21 trains per day in 1929. In other words, The Milwaukee Road had lost 57 percent of its passengers but could only shed 25 percent of its passenger trains.

A 1932 agreement with operating unions for a 10 percent wage rollback, and some government aid in the forms of loans from the Reconstruction Finance Corporation, were not enough to stem the tide of red ink that was engulfing the Milwaukee's financial statements.

Bankruptcy (Again)

In April 1935 the Milwaukee began to default on its debt obligations, and on June 29, 1935, the company filed its second bankruptcy petition in ten years. The board of directors had concluded that borrowing additional money to service its debt obligations was pointless; what was needed was "a readjustment of the present capital structure."

Derleth writes that the reorganization proceedings "rapidly became a protracted struggle for advantage among various interests." The first reorganization plan was filed with the ICC in January 1938 but it came to naught, as did a proposal to merge the company with competitor Chicago & North Western (which had filed for bankruptcy one day prior to the Milwaukee). The reorganization process would drag on for ten years from start to finish.

As if the company's financial tribulations were not enough, nature found ways to make matters even more trying for the company's employees and customers. In January 1936, severe blizzards struck the heart of the railroad, first in Iowa and Minnesota, then extending eastward. By February 1, according to the April 1936 issue of *The Milwaukee Magazine*, the road's Milwaukee terminal was "under one of the worst blockades in its history." Two days later, another blizzard hit Iowa and the Dakotas. It too moved eastward across the railroad, accompanied by subzero temperatures, and was followed by still another storm.

One of the towns affected by the storms was Lawler, Iowa (on the line between Marquette and Mason City), where a cut in the rolling countryside provided an opportunity for snow to drift in. An employee wrote of the situation at Lawler, "when an L-2 [Mikado] engine passes through the cut in the drift, the only thing that can be seen is the smoke coming out of the smokestack."

Flangers, wedge plows, and rotaries were all pressed into service to clear lines, but in late February another storm began. In the mid-1930s railroads provided a more important lifeline for rural communities than they do today, so the efforts of the Milwaukee and its employees (as well as other railroads in the region) to restore service garnered well-deserved accolades. The *Chicago American* newspaper summed it up this way: "The truly great achievement of the railroads in the cold spell has been keeping the population fed and warm."

In 1938, the Milwaukee's resilience would be tested by another crisis, also brought about by nature. On June 19, the piers on the bridge over Custer Creek, a normally dry creek bed near Saugus, Montana, were undermined by water from a localized but very severe storm. Train 15, the westbound *Olympian*, derailed as it passed over the weakened structure at an estimated 51 miles per hour (according to the account of former Milwaukee employee George Flynn, published in the First Quarter 2002 issue of *The Milwaukee Railroader*), derailing seven of its 11 cars. Of the 175 people on board, 47 died and 75 were injured.

In terms of casualties, this was the worst accident in the history of The Milwaukee Road. Employees responded quickly, decisively, and even heroically, and an ICC investigation found no fault with the railroad's maintenance or operating procedures, but it was costly to the railroad in terms of both money and reputation.

By 1939, traffic had recovered somewhat from the low levels of the early 1930s, but at $106.9 million, revenues were still far from what they had been a decade earlier. In its annual report for the year, the company reported, "beginning with the month of September, and lasting through October, there was a sharp upturn in traffic, which was handled without congestion or delay, demonstrating the capacity and ability of the railroad to meet successfully the demands upon it." The Milwaukee Road would soon have its capacity and ability put to a much more severe test.

Above: The winter of 1977 and 1978 was a challenging one for railroads in the Upper Midwest. Snowplow X900248 battles the white stuff south of Rockton, Illinois, on the line between Davis Junction, Illinois, and Janesville, Wisconsin, in January 1978. *Joe McMillan* Left: Plow X900248 was a good example of how the Milwaukee economized by recycling obsolete equipment. Originally a steam locomotive tender, it was modified by the railroad's own shop forces. *Joe McMillan*

Milwaukee 41, with cab units designated "A" and "D" and booster units "B" and "C," was the railroad's second 5,400-horsepower FT. Built in July 1943, it is shown here at the Electro-Motive plant in LaGrange, Illinois. *Photo by Electro-Motive Division of General Motors Corporation. Author collection*

CHAPTER FOUR

WORLD WAR II AND THE TRANSITION FROM STEAM TO DIESEL

The Milwaukee Road's Annual Report for 1941 began with these words: "Our country is at war. It is total war such as we have never known. Transportation is an indispensable part of war service. The Milwaukee Road knows this and is determined to discharge its full obligation which means intelligent, well-directed and unceasing effort in carrying forward its part of the war program."

Over the next four years, the Milwaukee would find itself taxed by an overabundance of business, a shortage of manpower as its employees

The Milwaukee Shops built virtually every type of equipment used on the railroad, including locomotives, passenger and freight cars, and cabooses. This company photo shows cabooses under construction in the shops. *Milwaukee Road Archives of the Milwaukee Public Library*

entered military service, and a shortage of equipment due to materials shortages and strict War Production Board guidelines on what types of rail equipment could be produced. The company summed up the situation in its 1942 annual report: "The loss of thousands of trained men to the armed forces and the shortage of critical materials, coupled with the greatest traffic volume in the history of the railroad, made 1942 a year of many difficulties."

Initially, the effect of greater traffic, spread over the railroad's relatively fixed cost structure, was to improve the efficiency of its operations. The operating ratio, which had stood at 81.1 percent in 1938, declined to 70.0 percent in 1941 and 64.6 percent in 1942. In the first phase of the war effort, the Milwaukee's productivity improved dramatically. Cars were used more efficiently: from 1938 to 1942, the ratio of empty to loaded freight car-miles dropped 10 percentage points, and average car-miles per day rose 60 percent. More trains were run (freight-train miles increased 27 percent). Each train carried more (net ton-miles per freight train-hour increased by 39.5 percent). These results were accomplished with a work force only 15 percent larger than in 1938.

By the end of 1943, 4,946 Milwaukee Road employees had entered the armed forces; by the end of 1945, that number had

America's Roads to Victory
are boulevards of steel and stamina

"Faster, faster," is wartime America's cry to the railroads. Speed the troop trains! Speed the supply and munitions trains! Speed the critical materials to the factories!

It's a challenge the railroads are taking in stride. They're coming through on every assignment, even though their need today is more new equipment than is available under existing priorities.

The railroads are mastering war traffic problems because they were ready with a modern plant that, in recent years, had been utilized to only half its capacity.

The Milwaukee Road, for example, prepared with new power as well as new freight and passenger cars, in the decade before war struck. It improved more than 2,000 miles of track with heavier rail and new ballast. It rebuilt over 80,000 lineal feet of bridges. It reduced curvatures to permit faster schedules... and 500 grade crossings were eliminated or provided with automatic protection.

These improvements, plus heavier tonnage on both cars and trains, account for The Milwaukee Road's present ability to double its load. Aided by the cooperation of business and government shippers, its 35,000 loyal, determined employees are ably handling their tremendous responsibilities.

The Milwaukee Road and the other railroads constitute one of our vital war industries.

CHICAGO MILWAUKEE ST. PAUL AND PACIFIC

THE MILWAUKEE ROAD
11,000-MILE SUPPLY LINE FOR WAR AND HOME FRONTS

A 1943 ad shows streamlined Class F7 Hudson 100 passing a train loaded with military tanks. Author collection

In the 1940s, General Motors produced a series of ads showing its customers' FT locomotives contrasted with stylized renditions of nineteenth-century locomotives. This ad, for the Milwaukee, shows the railroad's first road freight diesel, FT 40, which was initially assigned to service between Avery, Idaho, and Othello, Washington, in the gap between the electrified zones. *Author collection*

increased to 6,916, including 161 who died in military service. Milwaukee Road employees were the core of the 744th Railway Operating Battalion of the Army Transportation Corps, which was formed in 1943 and served in France and Germany until the end of the war in 1945.

But the Milwaukee's people knew that they were playing a vital role on the home front. The annual report for 1943 carried a photo captioned "Junior Manpower: High School boys who have helped greatly to meet the manpower shortage on extra gangs and sections crews." The cover of the 1944 report bore an illustration of a young track laborer staring wistfully at a formation of military aircraft flying overhead. It was titled "We Can't All Wear Wings." The caption said that the painting "conveys encouragement to young men who were disqualified for military service to perform railroad work, which is so vital to victory."

As profitable as The Milwaukee Road was, given the heavy wartime volumes, the company, like other U.S. railroads, felt that it was not being adequately compensated for its services, particularly in light of the pressure on wages during the war. In 1941, the railroads sought a 10 percent across-the-board rate increase, which the ICC approved but with a maximum increase of 6 percent and numerous exceptions. In its 1942 annual report, Milwaukee management said that it expected to improve its freight revenues by about $5.12 million as a result of the increase, based on 1941 business levels. ICC suspended the increase in 1943 after being in effect for only 14 months.

At the same time, three railway labor unions were threatening to strike if they did not get the wage increases they were seeking. This prompted the government to take control of the railroads in late December 1943, but the period of government control lasted less than a month. When the dust settled, the unions had wage increases, and the Milwaukee said that

the total cost of this round of increases (including "me too" increases granted to employees not represented by the striking unions) would be just over $10 million.

In the five years from 1938 to 1943, the number of ton-miles produced by The Milwaukee Road increased 115 percent, but its revenue per ton-mile declined by 1.5 percent. It was obvious that when the war ended, there would be a dramatic drop-off in freight tonnage. In the face of declining revenue yield, the operative question appeared to be whether the Milwaukee would be able to withstand the transition to peacetime.

As difficult as the war years were for the Milwaukee, and as much as management had to focus on the day-to-day task of keeping the railroad running under extremely heavy traffic, capital improvement projects that would enable it to operate more efficiently in the future were not ignored. In the early 1940s the line from Birmingham, Missouri, to Kansas City was rebuilt as a joint project with the Rock Island. This included construction of a new lift bridge across the Missouri River. Once the line went into operation in June 1945, Milwaukee set up a joint terminal operation at Kansas City with Kansas City Southern Railway. Also in the mid-1940s the Milwaukee installed centralized traffic control on several segments of its network with the objective of improving

The Milwaukee bought three General Electric 44-tonners in 1940 and 1941, but the little units never found a good long-term application on the railroad. No. 992 (originally 1701) is at Milwaukee in April 1966. It was traded in to EMD on a GP40 the following year. *Jim Scribbins*

MILW Class F6 Hudson 131 is in charge of the eastbound *Columbian* at Marshall, Washington, in 1950. *Photo by Philip Hastings, courtesy of California State Railroad Museum/ negative no. 3533*

traffic flow, enhancing safety, and increasing line capacity. By the end of 1945, 18 segments totaling 295 miles were under CTC operation.

The Postwar Era: A Difficult Start

Milwaukee Road shareholders had much to be pleased about in the 1945 annual report. Wartime hostilities had ended and the Milwaukee had emerged from bankruptcy on December 1, 1945. Freight revenues were off only 3 percent from the record levels of 1943, and returning troops had given an enormous boost to the company's passenger traffic. However, the operating ratio had been heading upward since the stellar performance of 1942 and 1943. In both of those years the operating ratio was below 65 percent, but it jumped six points in 1944, and in 1945 it stood at a worrisome 81.6 percent.

In early 1947, after recording an operating ratio of 85.4 percent the previous year, Milwaukee management noted that 1946, the first full year of postwar operations, had been marked by "a decline in gross revenues, shortages of materials, wage increases and higher costs of materials, including fuel." The wartime production limits on railcars resulted in shortages of many car types. Strikes by the Brotherhood of Railroad Trainmen and the Brotherhood of Locomotive Engineers, and federally mandated settlements with other rail unions, resulted in agreements that increased the company's labor costs by $16 million. There were also strikes in the industries the Milwaukee served, contributing to the loss of traffic and revenues, and in the coal mines, creating a shortage of fuel for the railroad's locomotives.

Discretionary maintenance was deferred both because of the company's reduced operating margins and because of a postwar shortage of rail. Materials shortages also impacted production programs at the Milwaukee Shops.

The photographer's notes for this October 1950 photo read: "Trains #103 and #102 meet midway of their respective trips between Bovill and St. Maries [Idaho]. N3 2-6-6-2 50 and C5a 2-8-0 1229 will both turn on the wye here and go back to their respective terminals. Logs and finished lumber are headed north on #102 to the CMStP&P main line at St. Maries, while empty log flats and box cars are going south to Bovill on #103. The N3 is needed south of here because of the heavy northbound grade, whereas the C5a will drop back down the St. Maries River valley with the northbound loads." *Photo by Philip Hastings, courtesy of California State Railroad Museum/negative no. 3836*

It was not an auspicious start for the postwar period. The Milwaukee would be challenged to bring its plant and equipment up to the standards necessary to serve its customers' needs, despite its decline in operating income, while at the same time facing new competitive challenges for both freight and passenger traffic.

Steam Locomotive Development

The evolution of steam power on The Milwaukee Road followed a pattern similar to that of many railroads, but as the design and construction of steam locomotives became more sophisticated in the twentieth century, specialization produced a distinctively "Milwaukee" fleet. According to William D. Edson's comprehensive all-time roster in *Railroad History* No. 136, steam locomotives of 11 distinct configurations saw road service on the Milwaukee:

- Class A 4-4-2 (Atlantic)
- Class B 4-6-0 (Ten-Wheeler) compound
- Class C 2-8-0 (Consolidation)
- Class F 4-6-2 (Pacific) and 4-6-4 (Hudson)
- Class G 4-6-0 simple
- Class H 4-4-0 (American)
- Class K 2-6-2 (Prairie)
- Class L 2-8-2 (Mikado)
- Class M 2-6-0 (Mogul)
- Class N 2-6-6-2 (Mallet)
- Class S 4-8-4 (Northern)

N3 Class 2-6-6-2 51 receives a steam cleaning at Spokane before taking train 291 north on the Metaline Falls Branch in September 1950. *Photo by Philip Hastings, courtesy of California State Railroad Museum/ negative no. 3153*

In addition, the company had three classes of steam locomotives built for yard service:
- Class D 0-8-0
- Class I 0-6-0
- Class J 0-4-0

Starting in the 1850s, the 4-4-0 American type was the most common locomotive on The Milwaukee Road and its predecessors. Construction of locomotives with this wheel arrangement continued at Milwaukee Shops through 1897. The 4-4-0 was supplanted as the mainstay of the fleet by the 4-6-0, or Ten-Wheeler. As Jim Scribbins notes in *Milwaukee Road Remembered*, the 4-6-0 was "well suited to the profiles and commodities of the St. Paul. Ten-Wheelers remained relatively plentiful on the road until dieselization."

The Milwaukee's 4-4-0's and 4-6-0's were used in both freight and passenger service, but from the 1900s forward, freight and passenger locomotives on the Milwaukee followed largely distinct paths of development. On the freight side, eight-coupled locomotives predominated. The Consolidation (2-8-0) was first used in 1901, followed by the Mikado (2-8-2) in 1909. Following completion of the Puget Sound extension in that year, Mikados were used in the mountainous territories of Montana, Idaho, and Washington. The ultimate development of steam power for freight service on the Milwaukee, however, was in the form of the Northern (4-8-4), which the railroad began to acquire in the 1930s.

Two notable exceptions to the dominance of eight-coupled power in freight service during the twentieth century were the Prairie (2-6-2) type and the road's 36 Class N 2-6-6-2 Mallets. Scribbins notes that after the western extension opened, the Prairie type was used to move freight between the Twin Cities and the Rockies. When the Mikados proved inadequate for the western lines' most rugged territory, the Mallets were introduced as helpers, with the first locomotive of this type being delivered by the American Locomotive Company (Alco) in December 1910.

In both the steam and diesel eras, the Milwaukee's choice of motive power was influenced by the high percentage of branchlines in its network. These lines' light rail was one factor that kept Ten-Wheelers and other light engines in service longer on the Milwaukee than on most other large railroads.

If eight-coupled steam power was the dominant factor on the Milwaukee's freight trains during the first half of the century, the equivalent on passenger trains was six-coupled power, notably the Pacific (4-6-2) and Hudson (4-6-4) types. But the golden age in the development of Milwaukee passenger locomotive began in 1935 with the introduction of the *Hiawatha*s and their distinctive streamlined Atlantic (4-4-2) locomotives—a wheel arrangement considered archaic by most other railroads in the mid-1930s.

In testing the concept of a high-speed passenger train, the Milwaukee used a Hudson on a July 1934 run that attained a top speed of 103.5 miles per hour between Chicago and Milwaukee. But the railroad was designing this service using a clean sheet of paper. Rather than adapt an existing locomotive, it requested proposals for a machine designed specifically for high-speed service. Alco was selected to build two new streamlined Atlantics. As Scribbins notes, they "were designed to pull six cars and proved capable of handling nine cars at sustained 90–100 mph speeds."

This specially developed automatic spot welder is welding steel plates that form the side of a box car.

Here the completed side of a box car has been hoisted into place and is being fastened to the floor frame.

From The Milwaukee Road's 1946 annual report, photos of work in progress at the Milwaukee Shops. *Author collection*

When the service was restructured in 1939, the *Morning Hiawatha* (trains 5 and 6) became heavier than the original *Hiawatha* consists had been, necessitating larger power. Thus was born the streamlined 4-6-4 Hudson (streamlining was also applied to 4-6-0 and 4-6-2 locomotives). Eventually, streamlined Milwaukee passenger engines could be found not just between Chicago and the Twin Cities but also in places like Green Bay, Sioux Falls, and Omaha.

Through the end of World War II, the Milwaukee remained a predominately steam-powered railroad. At the end of 1945, it had 1,022 steam locomotives on its roster: 550 freight, 170 passenger, and 302 yard. Steam locomotives generated 77 percent of its gross ton-miles in freight service that year, diesels 13 percent, and electrics 10 percent. But the Milwaukee was on the threshold of a ten-year conversion program that would bring an end to steam operations by 1957.

Early Diesels

Like most large railroads, the Milwaukee got its first experience with trains powered by internal combustion through its operation of self-propelled gas-electric railcars.

According to former Milwaukee Road engineer Bill Wilkerson, the railroad's first application of diesel power came in 1927, when one such car, built by General Electric in 1913, was converted to diesel. The company's first production internal combustion locomotives were a pair of gas-electric 325-horsepower Whitcomb center-cabs, the first delivered in late 1929 and the second in mid-1930. In 1941 they were converted to diesel-electric. Wilkerson reports that these units remained on the Milwaukee until 1944, when they were sold to the U.S. Navy.

In 1939 the Milwaukee took its first significant step in the direction of dieselizing its locomotive fleet with the acquisition of six switch engines. They consisted of two Alco high-hood, 600-horsepower units and four Electro-Motive Corporation (EMC) engines, two rated at 600 horsepower and two at 1,000 horsepower. The EMC models were both powered by EMC's 567 engine, which was used in new locomotives by EMC's successor, the Electro-Motive Division of General Motors Corporation, until the mid-1960s.

Over the next two years, through late 1941, the Milwaukee would continue to add

Class F6a Hudson 145 (formerly 6417) was constructed by Baldwin Locomotive Works in 1931 and is shown here in an undated photo at Milwaukee. *Milwaukee Road Archives of the Milwaukee Public Library*

Above: Milwaukee 1651 was one of the railroad's first six–diesel-electric locomotives. Built in 1939 by Electro-Motive Corporation, the 1651 was a 1,000-horsepower Model NW2. It remained in service until 1980. This undated photo shows the 1651 at Milwaukee Depot. *Milwaukee Road Archives of the Milwaukee Public Library* Right: In the early years of dieselization, the Milwaukee sampled the products of all the major builders of diesel locomotives. Although Baldwin switchers such as the 924 (an S12 delivered in 1950) never made up a very big part of the railroad's diesel roster, they could still be found working in the Twin Cities as late as the 1970s. Here, the 924 works the intermodal facility at St. Paul in 1970. *Stan Smaill*

to its roster of diesel switch engines, with a total of 70 placed into service. Most of these were Alco and EMD products, but a few units also came from Baldwin, Whitcomb, and General Electric. Wilkerson observes that the diesel switch engines' "ability to stay on outlying jobs for several days without service endeared them to management." But the biggest benefits of dieselization would be on the road, not in the yard. Steam locomotives required frequent fueling, watering, and lubrication. They had to be turned at the end of each run. They were labor-intensive machines.

The diesel that opened the eyes of skeptics throughout the rail industry (including those on the Milwaukee) to the potential of diesel road power, was Electro-Motive 103, the four-unit FT demonstrator set. As *TRAINS Magazine* observed, the impact of the FT on railroading was the same as "that of the jet upon aviation and the nuclear age

Top: Electro-Motive E6 15A-B was the Milwaukee's first diesel passenger locomotive, built in September 1941. It was successful enough that Milwaukee ordered five two-unit sets of its successor model, the E7, following World War II. Shown here at Milwaukee in an undated photo, the 15A-B were traded in to EMD for E9s in 1961. *Milwaukee Road Archives of the Milwaukee Public Library*
Above: The Milwaukee Road rostered only one set of Alco's DL109 passenger locomotive, the 14A-B, built in October 1941. The Otto Kuhler–designed nose and cab of the 14A were removed by Milwaukee shops in 1953, replaced by an EMD "bulldog" nose such as that found on E7 and F7 locomotives. Both the 14A and the 14B were scrapped at Milwaukee in the early 1960s. This undated photo was taken at Milwaukee Depot. *Milwaukee Road Archives of the Milwaukee Public Library*

Photographer Philip Hastings captured Milwaukee F7 110A next to the sanding tower at Savanna, Illinois, in December 1979. The 110A was scrapped two years later, in December 1981. *Milwaukee Road Archives of the Milwaukee Public Library*

upon the Navy." Each unit was rated at 1,350 horsepower.

Jim Scribbins, in his book, *The Milwaukee Road 1928–1985*, reports that on June 14, 1940, the FT demonstrator set departed from the Milwaukee's major Chicago-area yard at Bensenville, Illinois, with Time Freight 263 destined for Seattle, and that over the course of the run the demo set would handle as much as 7,000 tons. The Milwaukee's first four-unit FT set would be delivered in 1941.

Once diesels became common, they would roam their owners' systems, with little regard for geography. That wasn't the case in 1941; instead, diesel locomotives were acquired for specific applications. In the case of the Milwaukee's first FT, No. 40 (actually 40A-B-C-D), this meant several years of freight service in the gap between the two electrified zones, between Avery, Idaho, and Othello, Washington.

More FT locomotives followed over the next four years, and by mid-1945 the Milwaukee had 13 four-unit sets.

The ribbed sides that gave away any car—passenger or freight—as a product of Milwaukee Shops, are evident on coach 4574, in suburban service in August 1974. Train 131 is outbound at Western Avenue, Chicago, powered by E9 38A, a 1961 product of the Electro-Motive Division of General Motors. *Tom Murray*

Diesels were equally attractive for their potential in passenger service, and 1941 also saw the delivery of the company's first diesel passenger locomotives, a pair of Electro-Motive 2,000-horsepower E6 units, Nos. 15A-B, for service between Chicago and the Twin Cities. These, too, would become a standard-bearer for the Milwaukee, with five identical sets arriving over the next several years. In addition, one set of Alco's competitive product, the DL109 (numbered 14A-B), was received in November 1941. The economic appeal of the diesel in passenger service (as well as freight) was simple: the railroad could keep it in service almost continuously. In their first assignment, Milwaukee 15A-B would handle train 6, the *Morning Hiawatha*, from Minneapolis to Chicago. On arrival, it would turn back on train 57, the night mail train. In a 24-hour period it could generate 882 miles of revenue service.

Then there was the road switcher. Initially conceived as a roadworthy modification of the switch engine, with a short hood at one end that could accommodate a boiler for passenger service, the road switcher type would evolve into the standard North American freight locomotive. Milwaukee's first experience with this type of locomotive came with the 1941 acquisition of two Alco RS-1 1,000-horsepower road switchers for service on branchlines out of Spokane.

World War II brought limits on locomotive production. Because of the FT's success, EMD was the sole builder of diesel freight locomotives during the war, and as *TRAINS Magazine* noted, "the supply was strictly rationed." The Milwaukee, like other railroads, had to continue buying some steam locomotives, given the limited availability of diesels. In 1944, ten new S3 Class 4-8-4 freight locomotives, numbered 260 to 269, were added to the fleet, the last steam power delivered to The Milwaukee Road.

The Milwaukee Shops and Their Distinctive Cars

Five hundred 50-foot boxcars were constructed at the Milwaukee Shops in 1941, and orders were placed for 1,000 40-foot boxcars, 500

Given the favorable cost effects of being able to do extensive equipment rebuilding and upgrading in-house, rather than depending on outside contractors, the Milwaukee would often take an obsolete group of cars or locomotives and bring them up to modern standards. That's the case here, in the mid-1970s, as the railroad upgrades a group of log flats in the Milwaukee Shops. *Milwaukee Road Archives of the Milwaukee Public Library*

automobile cars, and 500 hopper cars. However, a War Production Board (WPB) order of 1942 froze new construction after only 600 of these cars (the 500 hoppers and 100 of the auto cars) had been completed. The WPB did authorize the Milwaukee to construct 735 gondolas and 400 flatcars during 1943. In 1944, more than 2,000 cars were built at the Milwaukee Shops.

The earmark of a freight or passenger car that had been built at Milwaukee Shops, beginning in the 1930s, was horizontal ribbing extending along the entire length of the carbody. John Grube, who worked at the Shops in the late 1970s, says, "The ribs resulted from an extensive program of research into new methods of car construction utilizing then-new high-tensile steels. It was found that the addition of these stiffening ribs allowed the use of much thinner gauge steels. All-welded construction was also introduced, eliminating the use of bolts and rivets that characterized older equipment. Along with new materials and techniques, new shop equipment was developed, including automatic spot and seam welders, wire-feed welders, and progressive dies to manufacture components for the new cars. Car sides, roofs, ends, and underframes were constructed in special fixtures, welded with the automatic equipment, and then brought together to form the new carbody. Many of the techniques and methods pioneered by The Milwaukee Road were later adopted by other builders."

In 1945, the Milwaukee began a $4.3-million modernization of the Milwaukee Shops. The shops, it said, had pioneered equipment such as "the all-welded, lightweight steel cars of the *HIAWATHAS*, and all-welded, steel, plywood-lined freight cars that carry heavier pay loads with less dead weight." But the buildings and layout were old. The modernization program would include "new passenger car and locomotive shops, a new storehouse and office building, provision for steel fabricating and forging facilities, and new covered craneway, and necessary changes in tracks and roadways within the shop area." In the coming years, the Milwaukee Shops would remain an important asset to The Milwaukee Road, enabling it to build new cars at a cost less than would have been required to buy them from commercial car builders, and allowing it to extend the life of both cars and locomotives through economical rebuilding and upgrading programs.

GP9 325 sits inside the engine house at St. Paul in the early 1970s, surrounded by diesel locomotive parts. *Mike Foley*

In January 1969, the operation of sleeping cars became the responsibility of individual railroads following the Pullman Company's exit from this business. In July of that year, The Milwaukee Road acquired *Pacific Guard* and four other sleepers from Union Pacific to cover its contribution to the Chicago–West Coast equipment pool. Here, *Pacific Guard* is relettered for its new owner at the Western Avenue coach yard in Chicago. *Phil Gosney*

CHAPTER FIVE

PASSENGER SERVICE

For most of its existence, The Milwaukee Road made the operation of a comprehensive network of passenger trains one of its highest priorities. In the company's earliest years, it could be assumed that virtually any line of railroad that had freight service would also have passenger service. This was, after all, an essential public service.

In 1880, 30 years after the first train operation by a CM&StP predecessor, passenger revenues represented $3.2 million in revenues for the company, or 24 percent of the total revenues for the year. Express and

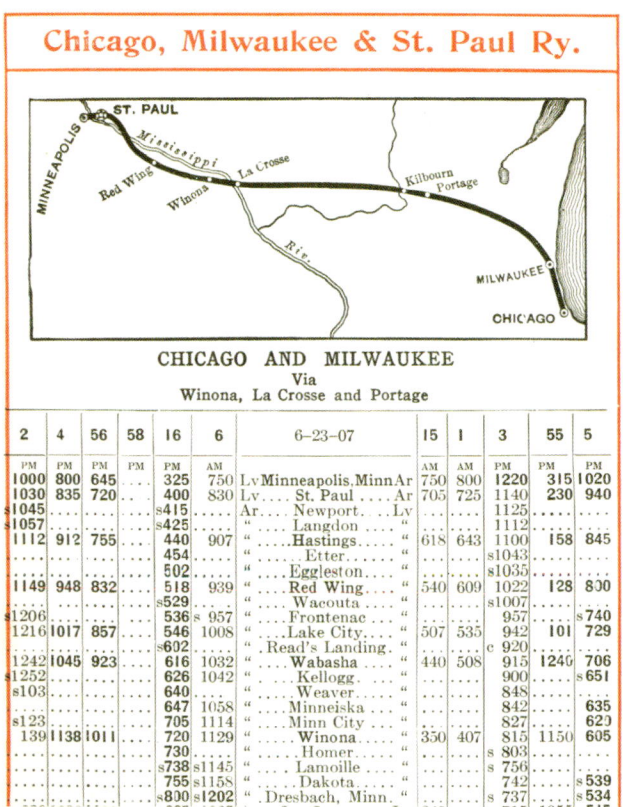
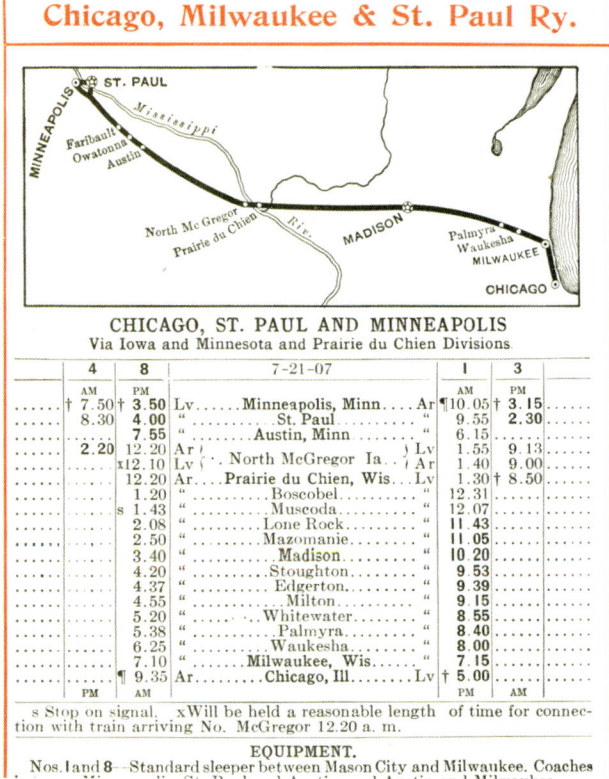

In the early twentieth century, each railroad tried to give travelers the impression that it had the most direct route between any two cities, so railroad maps took liberties with geography. The CM&StP, for example, had two routes between Chicago and the Twin Cities, but one was 80 miles longer than the other. The railroad solved the problem by relocating Madison and Prairie du Chien on their map so that the 502-mile route via those stations appeared almost equal in distance to the 422-mile route via La Crosse. *Milwaukee Road Archives of the Milwaukee Public Library*

mail services added another $1 million to the coffers. By 1888, passenger revenues had almost doubled to $6 million, or 35 percent of total revenues. In the fiscal year ending June 30, 1888, the railroad carried 7.9 million passengers. Thus, it is not surprising, in the company's *Local Time Tables* dated September 1, 1888, to find passenger trains listed on no fewer than 60 routes across the 5,577-mile system.

The marquee passenger route, then and for as long as The Milwaukee Road operated intercity passenger trains, was between Chicago, Milwaukee, St. Paul, and Minneapolis—"The Fast Mail Line," as it was known in 1888, thanks to the overnight train inaugurated in 1884 to carry mail between Chicago and St. Paul.

In 1888, there were two major passenger trains in each direction on the route. Train 1, departing Chicago at 5:30 p.m., was listed as a "vestibuled train" and included "Pullman Buffet Drawing Room Sleeping Cars (with smoking compartments)," as well as coaches between Chicago and Minneapolis, and parlor and dining cars between Chicago and Milwaukee. Its eastbound counterpart, train 4, departed Minneapolis at 6:50 p.m. Both trains operated on 14-hour-40-minute schedules from origin to destination. Trains 3 (departing Chicago at 10:30 p.m.) and 2 (departing Minneapolis at 2:20 p.m.) offered similar services, but did not offer vestibuled cars, and ran on 16-hour-plus schedules.

September 1888 marked the introduction of electric lighting on trains 1 and 4. In his book, *Milwaukee Road Remembered*, Jim Scribbins observes that this was the first use of electric lighting by any railroad west of Chicago. In 1898, trains 1 and 4 would be named the *Pioneer Limited*. The Milwaukee Road would continue to operate a train under this name (and these train numbers) on the Chicago–Twin Cities route until 1970.

Decades before the Milwaukee's passenger partnership with Union Pacific in the mid-1950s, the two railroads cooperated in the operation and promotion of through passenger service, as shown by this advertisement from the early twentieth century. *Author collection*

An illustration from a mid-1920s promotional booklet shows a Bi-Polar leading the *Olympian* through the Cascades. *Author collection*

In 1888, sleepers could also be found between:

- Chicago and
    - Omaha, Nebraska
    - Sioux City, Iowa
    - Dubuque, Iowa
    - Marion, Iowa
    - Prairie du Chien, Wisconsin
- St. Paul and Minneapolis and
    - Savanna, Illinois
    - North McGregor, Iowa (later renamed Marquette)
    - Aberdeen, Dakota Territory
- Madison, Wisconsin, and Sanborn, Iowa (via North McGregor)
- La Crosse, Wisconsin, and Fulda, Minnesota

Elsewhere on the railroad, the level of service varied considerably. The seeds of the railroad's Chicago suburban service had already been planted, with 16 weekday local trains between Chicago and Evanston (a line that would later be operated by the Chicago, North Shore & Milwaukee Railway and ultimately by the Chicago Transit Authority), and six between Chicago and Dunning, on a

spur off the line to Bensenville and Elgin. Many branchlines, however, saw but a single passenger train in each direction daily.

The trains best remembered today are the Milwaukee's "name" trains that provided sleeping, dining, parlor car, and lounge services, in addition to that more prosaic form of travel: coach. Some of the notable name trains initiated by CM&StP in the years prior to 1928 included:

- The *Arrow*, between Chicago and Omaha, with a section operating from Manilla to Sioux City, Iowa, and Sioux Falls, South Dakota;
- The *Copper Country Limited*, operated by CM&StP (via the former Milwaukee

Train 18, the eastbound *Columbian*, crosses the Spokane River at Spokane in March 1951. *Photo by Philip Hastings, courtesy of California State Railroad Museum/negative no. 3172*

The 1947 *Olympian Hiawatha* benefited from the expertise of industrial designer Brooks Stevens, who assisted with the design not only of cars but also the locomotive nose shield, as shown here on Erie-built No. 8. The stainless-steel shields were fabricated at the Milwaukee Shops and applied after the locomotives were delivered. Fairbanks-Morse's selling point for its line of locomotives was the Opposed Piston engine, which used two pistons in each cylinder. Originally developed for use in submarines, the O-P engine's advantage was supposed to be its reliability, but in railroad applications reliability proved to be an elusive goal. Today, Fairbanks-Morse Engine continues to build O-P engines at Beloit, Wisconsin, for marine and other uses. *Author collection*

& Northern) to Champion, Michigan, and operated beyond that point to Calumet and Marquette by the Duluth, South Shore & Atlantic Railway;

• The *Sioux*, between Chicago, Canton (Sioux Falls) and Rapid City, South Dakota;

• The *Pacific Limited*, between Chicago and Omaha, with cars operated beyond that point to Los Angeles (via Union Pacific) and Oakland (via Union Pacific to Ogden and Southern Pacific beyond); and

• The *Southwest Limited*, between Chicago (later Milwaukee) and Kansas City, Missouri.

With the exception of the *Pacific Limited*, all of these services lasted until the post–World War II era. However, the two Milwaukee Road passenger services that have been most widely written about, and will probably remain best remembered, are the *Olympian* and the *Hiawatha*s.

The *Olympian*

Trains 15 and 16, the *Olympian*, between Chicago and Seattle/Tacoma, debuted in May 1911, two years after the Puget Sound extension was completed. In his book, *More Classic Trains*, Arthur Dubin writes that the *Olympian* was "composed exclusively of railroad-owned and -operated equipment beautifully painted yellow-orange with maroon trim and gold lining." The electric-lighted cars were "finished on the interior with expensive carved hardwoods."

A September 1913 timetable shows the *Olympian* departing Chicago at 10:15 p.m. On its first day out, it arrived at Minneapolis at 11:30 a.m. and at Aberdeen, South Dakota, at 8:12 p.m. The next day would find it arriving at Miles City, Montana, at 6:34 a.m., and Butte at 7:15 p.m. On the final day of its westward journey, it arrived at Seattle at 8:00 p.m. and Tacoma at 9:30 p.m. Eastward, it departed Tacoma at 8:45 a.m.; three days and 2,201.2 miles later, it arrived in Chicago at 11:59 a.m.

Equipment consisted of an "observation car with library, smoking room, buffet, barber shop and bath," as well as "drawing room, compartment and standard sleeping cars, tourist sleeping cars, dining cars and coaches."

The *Olympian* was not the only train on the Puget Sound route. At the same time that it was inaugurated, the CM&StP also launched trains 17 and 18, the *Columbian*, on a schedule three hours slower than the *Olympian*, and with somewhat fewer amenities. Scheduled to depart from Chicago at 10:10 a.m. and from Tacoma at 5:45 p.m., it provided a more convenient schedule for stations served by the *Olympian* in the dead of night. Dubin writes that "twenty complete train consists—the first ones of steel construction to operate between Chicago and the Northwest—were required to equip the *Olympian* and the *Columbian*."

Electrification of the route through the mountains of Montana, Idaho, and Washington provided the railroad with a marketing advantage that it exploited to maximum advantage. A 1925 advertising brochure, *Pacific Northwest-The Wonderland*, describes the benefits to the passenger of being "in a palatial steel train drawn by a huge electric locomotive, the mightiest in the world. There is a uniformity of speed uphill and down grade with entire freedom from jerks, jolts and jars . . . and he feels further secure in the knowledge that the power of this engine is equal to that of several steam locomotives . . . So-called mountain grades are leveled and the motion of the train is even and sustained." Open-air observation cars were attached to the train during the summer months to give passengers the full benefit of the scenery—free, the brochure noted, from "cinders, smoke and soot."

One manifestation of The Milwaukee Road's independent streak was its on-again, off-again relationship with the Pullman Company, which operated sleeping and other

The Fairbanks-Morse Erie-builts were so named because they were assembled under contract by General Electric at its Erie, Pennsylvania, plant. The initial Erie-builts had chrome plating on the noses of the cab units, but MILW 22B, shown here in an undated photo at Milwaukee Shops, was among those without the chrome. The Erie-built carbody was styled by industrial designer Raymond Loewy. *Milwaukee Road Archives of the Milwaukee Public Library*

In an illustration from a 1956 promotional booklet, the westbound *Olympian Hiawatha* departs Chicago. Author collection

extra-service cars for most U.S. railroads. The first *Olympian* contained some Pullman-built cars, but they were operated by the railroad itself. In 1927, the train received new cars with lounges and sleepers operated by Pullman. In *Milwaukee Road Remembered*, Scribbins writes, "the Pullmans had Spanish-style interiors, at the time very much in vogue. All berths had coil spring mattresses."

In the 1920s and early 1930s, the running time of the *Olympian* was cut several times. A 1933 timetable shows running times of 60 hours, 45 minutes westbound and 59 hours eastbound. By this time, the *Olympian* was the only remaining transcontinental train in the Milwaukee's timetable. The *Columbian* was discontinued in 1931, although it would be revived as a Chicago–Tacoma train from 1947 to 1955.

In the decade following World War II, many long-distance passenger trains received new, lightweight equipment. The *Olympian*

In 1948 and 1949, railroads banded together to produce the "Chicago Railroad Fair" to celebrate the rich history of the industry and to show off its newest equipment. The fair coincided with the delivery of the final cars to streamline the *Olympian Hiawatha*, including the Skytop Lounge cars (which also went into service on the *Hiawatha*s between Chicago and the Twin Cities). The Milwaukee produced this illustration for an ad to promote both the fair and the new equipment. *Author collection*

was one of the first, and when the train's new coach, dining, baggage, café, and Touralux (economy) sleeping cars made their debut in 1947, it was renamed the *Olympian Hiawatha*. Initially, the new train's consist included older first-class sleeping cars, but by early 1949 the reequipping process was completed with the addition of the unique Skytop eight-bedroom observation lounge cars.

Both coming and going the *Olympian Hiawatha* presented an unmistakable image. It was hauled by Fairbanks-Morse Erie–built locomotives with distinctive stainless steel panels on the nose of the lead unit. On the rear was a *Creek*-series solarium observation car, with the Skytop Lounge featuring glass panels that permitted a panoramic view. The train got its finishing touch in 1952 with the arrival of full-length Super Dome cars.

The *Olympian Hiawatha* was, however, one of the earliest victims of the changing

The Milwaukee used this illustration to show the 360-degree view available from the Skytop Lounge observation car. Designer Brooks Stevens said in an article in the Third Quarter 1997 issue of *The Milwaukee Railroader* that "the illusion of compound curves was accomplished by piecing together flat window sections, which had to be fitted together like the facets of a diamond in a diamond ring." *Author collection*

Skytop parlor observation car 186, *Cedar Rapids*, gets a final, detailed wash from a laborer at Chicago's Western Avenue coach yard in August 1969; it will bring up the rear of train 3 from Chicago to Minneapolis later this day. The Skytop cars saw their last Milwaukee Road service on the *Afternoon Hiawatha*. Phil Gosney

economics of long-distance rail passenger service. It was discontinued as a Chicago–Tacoma train in 1961, with its memory perpetuated for a time in the form of an unnamed Minneapolis–Butte/Deer Lodge train that ran as trains 15 and 16. The train was cut back to Minneapolis–Aberdeen in 1964, and was terminated in 1969.

The *Hiawathas*

The mid-1930s were a period of innovation in the technology, operation, and marketing of the passenger train, prompted by an alarming decline in rail passenger patronage (which in turn was driven both by the Depression and by a rapid increase in automobile usage) and by the availability of new technologies.

The twin goals of the designers, engineers, operators, and promoters behind the innovations of this period were speed and the perception of speed. These were not always the same thing, although The Milwaukee Road managed to attain both goals. Speed was quantifiable, a matter of engineering and operation, and was achieved largely through lightweight cars propelled by locomotives specially designed for fast passenger service. The perception of speed was more a matter of design—specifically, the streamlining of locomotives and cars—and marketing.

The Chicago–Twin Cities corridor proved an ideal test bed for various approaches to the need for speed. The route had three railroads whose physical characteristics were suitable for fast passenger service: Chicago & North Western (C&NW); Chicago, Burlington & Quincy (CB&Q); and The Milwaukee Road.

C&NW was first out of the gate with its *400* service in January 1935, its name derived from the approximate mileage

Like other western railroads, the Milwaukee took advantage of its proximity to national parks and other scenic wonders to promote patronage on its passenger trains. Often, the railroads' marketing strategy went beyond advertising to include investments in facilities, like the Milwaukee's Gallatin Gateway Inn near Yellowstone, which opened in 1927. The stretch Fords shown here were used to shuttle passengers from the *Olympian* at Three Forks. Buses then took them to the park itself. *Milwaukee Road Archives of the Milwaukee Public Library*

between Chicago and St. Paul and the number of minutes that the train was allowed to traverse the route. The *400* initially used rebuilt Pacific-type steam locomotives and heavyweight cars. (In 1939, it would be reequipped with diesels and lightweight cars.) Despite the traditional style of its equipment, the C&NW had raised the bar for rail passenger service in the corridor.

CB&Q took a radically different approach. After a test run of the diesel-powered, fixed-consist *Zephyr*, No. 9900, between Chicago and St. Paul in July 1934, the railroad ordered two additional three-unit sets from their builder, the Budd Company of Philadelphia. They were dubbed the *Twin Zephyrs* and were placed into revenue service in April 1935. Dubin writes, "public acceptance of the trains was so enthusiastic that just 6 weeks later the service was doubled—by each train making a daily round trip." Less than two years later, they were replaced by similar seven-unit consists, with an eighth car added soon thereafter.

True to its independent ways, The Milwaukee Road entered the race not with recycled equipment, like the C&NW, nor with an articulated diesel-powered trainset like the CB&Q, but with completely new lightweight cars, built in its own shops. They were, Scribbins notes, "the first full-size all-welded streamlined coaches on any railroad."

A brochure distributed prior to the May 1935 inauguration of the *Hiawatha*. Author collection

A company postcard showing the first *Hiawatha* illustrates how its design elements were intended to make it appear as a unified entity, not simply a locomotive with cars. *Author collection*

The six-car consist would include a "Beaver Tail" parlor observation and a "Tip Top Tap" lounge car plus four coaches.

In another departure from the course pursued by many other railroads in the mid-1930s, the Milwaukee cast its lot not with internal combustion but with steam power. In its own way, the railroad made a radical choice of motive power by going with the 4-4-2 Atlantic, a type that had fallen out of favor elsewhere in the rail industry. Scribbins observes that "only steam was deemed capable of pulling the train to which CMStP&P was firmly committed: a full-size, non-articulated train." The American Locomotive Company (Alco) was chosen to build the engines, numbered 1 and 2, designated Class A according to the Milwaukee's locomotive classification scheme. Eventually, four such engines, Nos. 1 through 4, would grace the Milwaukee's steam roster.

Although some railroads had experimented with streamlining of steam locomotives, earlier efforts had all involved the installation of shrouding on conventionally designed engines. Engines 1 and 2, by contrast, were designed and built with streamlining,

It's the evening of January 30, 1963, and train 10, the *Copper Country Limited*, is stopped at Houghton, Michigan, on the Soo Line, en route to Champion, where it will reach Milwaukee Road trackage for the rest of its trip to Iron Mountain, Green Bay, Milwaukee, and Chicago. This train provided a link to the outside world for many small communities in the Upper Peninsula of Michigan and northern Wisconsin. It also served an important function by carrying mail to and from these towns, and featured a full working Railway Post Office between its end points of Calumet and Chicago. *Bob Anderson*

and were painted to match the orange-and-maroon scheme of the passenger cars.

Construction of cars and locomotives was well along before a name was settled on for the new service in April 1935: *Hiawatha*. In his book documenting the history of this train and its progeny, *The Hiawatha Story*, Scribbins writes that four Milwaukee employees suggested the name, as did an Alco official: "The legendary Indian was fleet of foot, as the train would be, and characters in Henry Wadsworth Longfellow's poem 'The Song of Hiawatha' could be associated with the city of Winona (Wenonah), Minn., and with Minnehaha Falls in Minneapolis."

Despite the competition from C&NW and CB&Q, the inauguration of *Hiawatha* service on May 29, 1935, with one daily train in each direction, was met with immediate and overwhelming success. The train grew from six cars initially to seven and, by August, to eight. In October 1936, the train was reequipped, growing to nine cars. In September 1938, a third incarnation of *Hiawatha* equipment took to the rails, and in January 1939, the service frequency was increased to two departures in each direction daily. The new *Morning Hiawatha* service included a Railway Post Office (RPO) car and was hauled by the successor to engines 1 and 2: streamlined Class F7 4-6-4 Hudson types.

The breakthrough represented by the *Hiawatha*s can be appreciated by comparing the Milwaukee's fastest Chicago–Minneapolis schedules before and after the inauguration of the *Hiawatha*s. In May 1933, for example, the fastest train on the route was the *Day Express*, trains 5 and 6. It consumed approximately 11

Two of the Milwaukee's five FP45 passenger locomotives power a 15-car ski special at Iron Mountain, Michigan, on February 1, 1970. From the photographer's notes: "Although common in earlier years, by the 1960s the ski train from Chicago or Milwaukee was down to about once a winter, commonly in late January. These would run Friday night northbound, for Saturday morning arrival around 6 A.M. Skiers could then get breakfast and head for the slopes at Pine Mountain on the north side of Iron Mountain. They would stay overnight at local hotels and motels. The train was run to Channing, turned on the wye, and serviced. Sunday afternoon about 3 or 4 P.M. the train left Iron Mountain for its run back to Milwaukee and Chicago. Typical consists were coaches and a couple of baggage cars for luggage and skis." *Bob Anderson*

hours in each direction. Trains 100 and 101, the *Hiawatha*s, needed only seven hours to complete the 421-mile journey, averaging 60 miles per hour, with seven intermediate stops.

The *Hiawatha*s were the signature trains of the Milwaukee's intercity fleet until the advent of Amtrak in 1971. They were dieselized in stages between 1941 and 1946. Beaver Tail parlor cars gave way to Skytop Lounge cars in the years after World War II, and in 1953 full-length Super Dome cars appeared in the consists.

Throughout the 1950s and 1960s, the railroad continued to operate two *Hiawatha*s from each end of the corridor daily. The *Morning Hiawatha* was an early morning departure from Minneapolis, with mid-afternoon arrival in Chicago, while its westbound counterpart was a midmorning departure from the Windy City and late-afternoon arrival in the Twin Cities. The Chicago times allowed easy connections with the eastern railroads' trains to and from Boston, New York, Philadelphia, and Washington, D.C. It survived until Amtrak took over the railroad's intercity services in May 1971.

The *Afternoon Hiawatha*s departed each city in early afternoon, allowing passengers to enjoy a leisurely dinner in the dining car before their evening arrival. Scribbins observes that it remained "a quality conveyance" until its final run on January 21, 1970.

A ski special is shown at Iron Mountain, Michigan, on January 30, 1971. The photographer reported that freight unit 5001 had been added as a result of problems with the train's FP7-E9B-FP7 locomotive consist. *Bob Anderson*

Regional Services

Hiawatha became not just a designation for the Milwaukee's premier train service between Chicago and the Twin Cities, but a brand name that was applied on other routes as well. In fact, it did not take long for the *Hiawatha* name to appear elsewhere in the Milwaukee's timetable. These offspring of *Hiawatha* had equipment reflecting their lineage, often because it was cascaded to these services, as the original trains were reequipped.

The *North Woods Hiawatha* came into existence in June 1936, serving the line from New Lisbon, Wisconsin, north to Wausau, Minocqua, and Star Lake, powered by a 4-6-0 (No. 10) in shrouding similar to that of the Class A engines. A second streamlined 4-6-0 (No. 11) was later assigned to the train from Wausau north.

Scribbins notes, "beginning in 1939 the *North Woods* was operated as a mainline train in the summer and during holiday periods between New Lisbon and Chicago (except in 1943). From 1951 on, Chicago operation was limited to weekends." Over the years, the train went through various changes in equipment and operating configuration. They lost the *Hiawatha* name in 1956 and were discontinued in 1970.

The *Midwest Hiawatha* ran between Chicago and Omaha, with a section splitting off at Manilla, Iowa, for Sioux City, Iowa, and Sioux Falls, South Dakota. One link to their *Hiawatha* parentage was the initial power for these trains, which were inaugurated in 1940: Class A 4-4-2s. The Sioux Falls section, Scribbins says, "was first powered by gaudily painted F5 Pacifics, then by a pair of 4-6-2s shrouded and painted in the style of the F7 Hudsons." The *Midwest Hiawatha* received new equipment in 1948, and was eventually dieselized. When the Milwaukee began handling Union Pacific's streamliners between Omaha and Chicago, the *Midwest Hiawatha* became two Sioux Falls coaches

91

In July 1970, Milwaukee train 203, the remnant of what had once been the *North Woods Hiawatha*, is viewed at New Lisbon, Wisconsin, from its connecting train, number 3, the *Afternoon Hiawatha* from Chicago to Minneapolis. *Steve Patterson*

appended to the *Challenger* east of Manilla. This remnant of the *Midwest Hiawatha* service was phased out in April 1956.

The *Chippewa* was the third regional service to take on the *Hiawatha* brand name. It was a Chicago–Green Bay–Ontonagon, Michigan, service, operated as trains 14 and 21. In 1948, it was reequipped with 1938 Beaver Tail parlor cars as well as new coaches, diners, and RPO-express cars, and was reborn as the *Chippewa-Hiawatha*. It was dieselized in 1950. Over time, the train took on local stops, and dining and parlor car services were downgraded. The *Hiawatha* name fell by the wayside in early 1957, and the train was discontinued in 1960.

However, there was more to The Milwaukee Road passenger timetable than the *Hiawatha*s. A sampling of trains from an April 1949 timetable includes:

- The *Varsity* between Madison and Chicago by way of Janesville and Walworth, Wisconsin;
- The *On Wisconsin* between Madison and Milwaukee;
- The *Tomahawk* between Minocqua, Wisconsin, and New Lisbon, with connecting service to Chicago; and
- The *Marquette* between Mason City, Iowa, and Chicago.

In addition, longtime stalwarts of the road's passenger fleet such as the *Pioneer Limited*, the *Arrow*, the *Copper Country Limited*, the *Sioux*, and the *Southwest Limited* continued to operate in the postwar era.

Partnership with Union Pacific

In the mid-1950s, Union Pacific was in an enviable position. At its eastern gateway,

Omaha, and across the Missouri River, at Council Bluffs, Iowa, were seven railroads ready to forward UP's traffic eastward: Chicago & North Western; Chicago, Burlington & Quincy; Chicago Great Western; Chicago, Milwaukee, St. Paul & Pacific; Chicago, Rock Island & Pacific; Illinois Central; and the Wabash. Of these, the North Western had long had the best relationship with UP. Not only did C&NW enjoy the most freight of any of the Omaha–Chicago roads, it also hosted UP's passenger streamliners to Denver, Portland, Oakland (where passengers transferred to ferries to reach San Francisco), and Los Angeles. But in the early 1950s, C&NW was deferring maintenance. In 1955, it paid the price.

As historian Richard Saunders explains in his book, *Merging Lines: American Railroads 1900–1970*, "that was the year UP summarily canceled its contract with the North Western to forward its West Coast passenger trains to Chicago. The North Western was constantly late delivering the trains to UP . . . The

In June 1950, the *Midwest Hiawatha* departs from Omaha, Nebraska, led by E7 18B. *Don Sims*

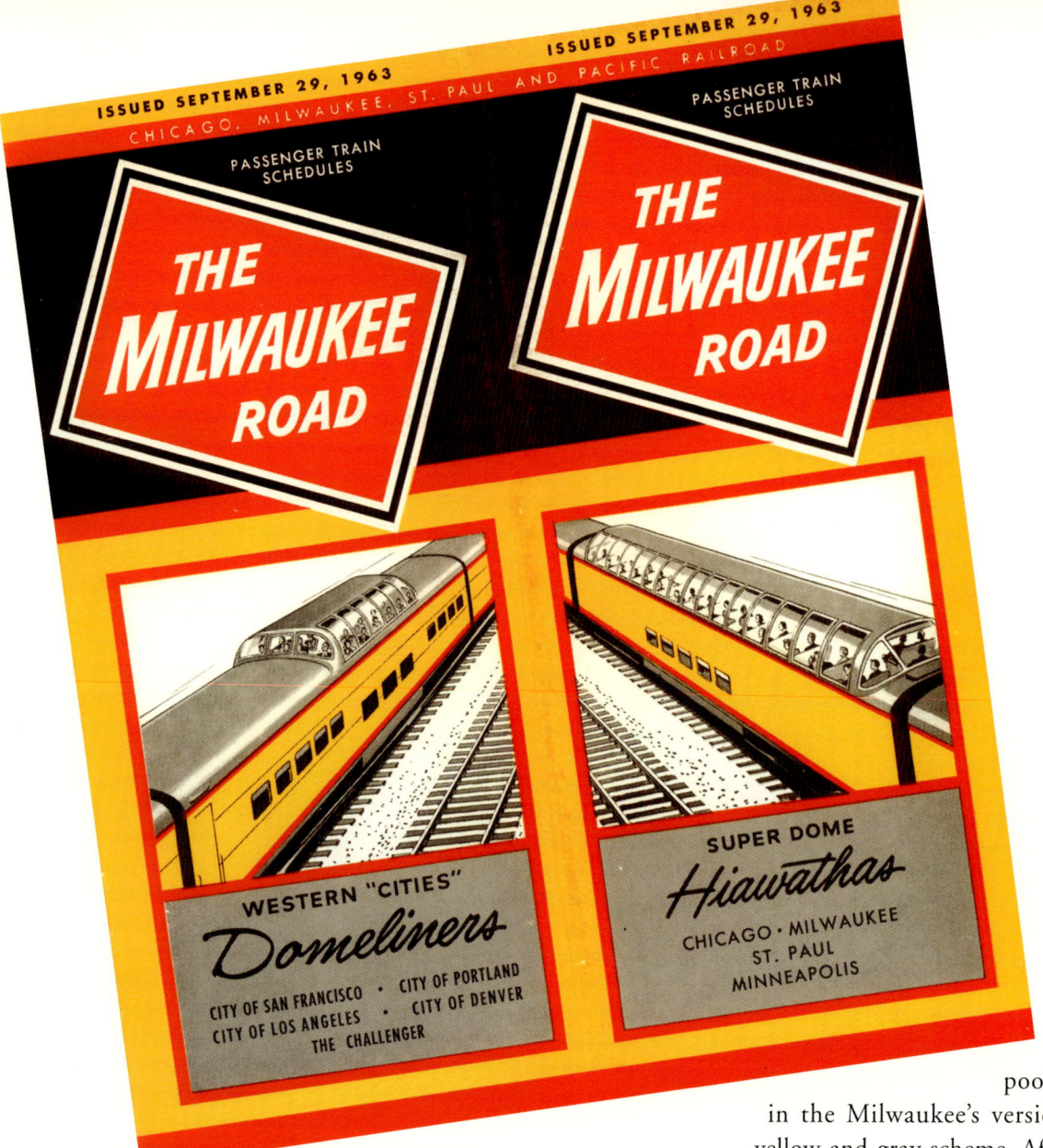

The Milwaukee Road's September 1963 passenger timetable shows the railroad's adaptation of the Union Pacific paint scheme. *Author collection*

Milwaukee Road got the passenger contract and hoped it would get the freight. It invested a lot of money to bring its Omaha Line up to speed, and it did not do so just for some passenger trains of dubious profit potential."

Although most of the freight stayed on the C&NW, the Milwaukee made a number of changes to integrate the UP *City of* trains (*Denver*, *Los Angeles*, *San Francisco*, and *Portland*) and the Chicago–Los Angeles *Challenger* into its preexisting passenger operations. Several train numbers, including those of the *Afternoon Hiawatha* (trains 100 and 101) were changed to avoid conflicts with UP's. The cars assigned to the *City* equipment pool were painted in the Milwaukee's version of the UP's yellow-and-gray scheme. After finding that this color scheme was more durable and easily maintained, the Milwaukee adopted the yellow color for all of its passenger trains, an effect that could still be seen on Milwaukee Road business cars and on some passenger equipment in suburban service long after the *City* trains had ended.

The *Challenger* was eventually discontinued and the *City* trains consolidated into a single train east of Omaha, unofficially known as the *City of Everywhere*. When Amtrak came into existence, it selected the CB&Q to host its Chicago–Oakland train, and the Santa Fe for its Chicago–Los Angeles service, bringing an end to intercity passenger service on The Milwaukee Road's Omaha route.

Train 104, the eastbound streamliner operated jointly by Milwaukee and Union Pacific, and known informally as the *City of Everywhere*, is about an hour from its destination, Chicago, as it passes through Elgin, Illinois, in October 1969. The *City* train often operated with as many as 23 cars on this portion of its route. *Phil Gosney*

The consolidated Milwaukee–Union Pacific *City of Denver/City of Portland*, train 111, heads into the sunset at Forreston, Illinois, in July 1969, with an FP7 and an FP45 for power. The photographer, who was working as the head brakeman on an eastbound freight, notes that "the ballast was nonexistent, the trackage was covered in a sea of green grass, and the riding was a bit rough." *Phil Gosney*

As they departed Union Station in Chicago, Milwaukee suburban trains passed under their Chicago & North Western counterparts. This midday, single-car train is leaving Chicago in August 1968. *Steve Patterson*

CHAPTER SIX

MODERNIZING THE RAILROAD:
The 1950s and 1960s

If 1946 was a transition year for The Milwaukee Road, then 1947 was the first full year of the postwar period on the railroad. It also marked a handover of the executive reins from Harry A. Scandrett, who since 1928 had served as president, trustee, and then president again, to Charles H. Buford. When he became president of the Milwaukee in May 1947, Buford was 61 years old. He was an up-from-the-ranks operating man who had served with the Association of American Railroads from 1939 to 1946, but had otherwise spent his entire career with the Milwaukee.

Alco road switcher 466, model RS3, was delivered to the Milwaukee in November 1955. Here it awaits a yard or local assignment at the Wausau, Wisconsin, engine facility, in August 1968. *Bob Anderson*

One accomplishment of the Buford years was the December 31, 1948, absorption of the company's Indiana Line. In 1921, the Chicago, Terre Haute & Southeastern Railway Company had been leased by the Milwaukee for 999 years. Consolidating the 197-mile subsidiary with the parent company, management said, would simplify accounting, tax, and corporate procedures and improve its ability to refinance CTH&S bonds in the future.

Buford's tenure as president of the Milwaukee was a short one, just over three years. John P. Kiley, 55 years old, succeeded Buford in September 1950. Kiley joined the Milwaukee in the engineering department in 1915 and had worked for the railroad continuously except for military duty during World War I.

The year 1950 was the centennial of the Milwaukee's oldest predecessor road, the Milwaukee & Mississippi (originally the Milwaukee & Waukesha). To celebrate the event, the Milwaukee sponsored meetings across the railroad to remind local communities of its long record of service and to spread the word about its plans for the future. On November 20 it staged a re-creation of the original 5-mile run from Milwaukee to Wauwatosa. On February 25, 1951, the company sent a special train to Waukesha to mark the 100th anniversary of the first operation from Milwaukee to that city.

New Equipment, New Yards

Much work had to be accomplished to restore the physical condition of the railroad after the war. Equipment was a particular problem. The Milwaukee faced a choice: should it put resources into new cars or should it improve the condition of the cars it already had? Initially, it went with new. The Milwaukee Shops built 1,200 gondolas, 331 40-foot boxcars, 65 all-steel cabooses, and 35 covered hoppers—a total of 1,631 cars—in 1946. The following year, the Shops delivered 1,454

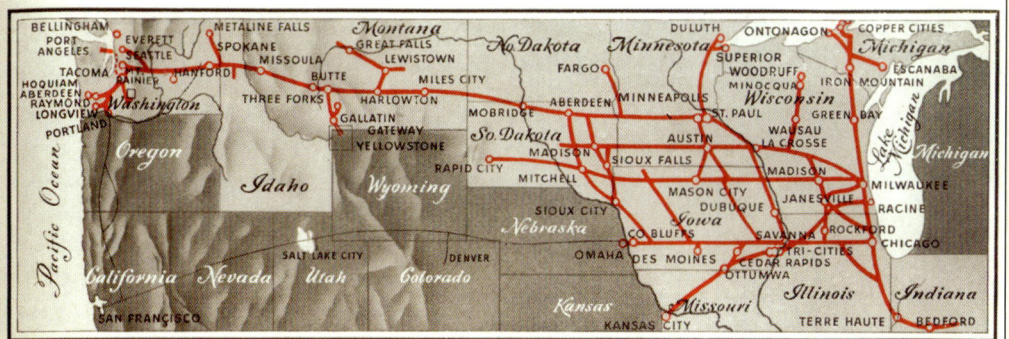

10,685 Miles of Main Line in 1947

At the end of 1947 The Milwaukee Road operated 10,685 miles of line in twelve states—touching two others. With additional main tracks, yard tracks and sidings, the total trackage operated was 15,970 miles.

Equipment

The equipment to operate this trackage consisted of:

LOCOMOTIVES		FREIGHT CARS		PASSENGER CARS	
Steam	1,027	Box and auto	29,964	Sleeping	83
Diesel road	52	Gondola and hopper	11,042	Coaches	373
Diesel switch	87	Flat	4,920	Parlor	37
Electric	49	Other	6,393	Baggage, mail and express	413
				Other	127
Total	1,215	Total	52,319	Total	1,033
				Rail motor cars	15

Above: MILW 74C, leading a freight at Franksville, Wisconsin, was delivered in 1949 in the Milwaukee's gray-and-orange diesel paint scheme, still worn by the booster unit in the middle of this three-unit consist. By June 1960, when this photo was taken, the 74C had been repainted in the simplified scheme of orange, maroon, and black; future simplification would eliminate the maroon stripe. This unit was part of a group of 36 traded in for new locomotives in 1965. *Bob Anderson* Left: A simplified map of The Milwaukee Road, and a summary of its equipment, from the company's 1947 annual report. *Author collection*

Above: In September 1950, N3 2-6-6-2 58 rolling northward on the Metaline Falls Branch near Dalkena, Washington. *Photo by Philip Hastings, courtesy of California State Railroad Museum/ negative no. 3120*

Right: For decades, it was not uncommon for a Class 1 railroad to cross the lines of interurban electric railways. That's the case here, in May 1952, as Milwaukee HH600 1602 waits for a Waterloo, Cedar Falls & Northern car at Cedar Rapids, Iowa. *Collection of Jim Scribbins*

freight cars (a mix of 40- and 50-foot boxcars and automobile cars) and 112 passenger cars.

In 1948, the new-car program continued at a very heavy pace. The Shops produced 2,800 gondolas, 2,781 40-foot boxcars, and 300 skeleton flatcars for log-loading, as well as 76 passenger cars. But by that year, the Milwaukee could also turn its attention to older cars. It explained that year's jump in equipment maintenance expense to shareholders as follows: "Railroad equipment was used to its maximum capacity during the war

This photo of the yardmaster's office at Air Line Yard in Milwaukee was part of a June 1952 release by the company's news bureau, publicizing the yard's $3 million upgrading. The photo caption reads in part: "Yardmaster's office is on the second floor of the tower. Microphone in his right hand is for radio communication with engine crews; the microphone over his desk is for paging and talk-back speakers located throughout the yard. Teletype in foreground is for transmission of train make-up and other information." *Milwaukee Road Archives of the Milwaukee Public Library*

years when, due to lack of experienced railroad labor and scarcity of materials, the maintenance program lagged considerably. Then, because of the extensive car building program at Milwaukee shops in 1946 and 1947, when there was not sufficient shop capacity to construct cars and carry on the maintenance work, the situation was further aggravated so that there was a considerable backlog of maintenance work accumulated that had to be carried out in 1948."

The new cars built by Milwaukee Shops in the late 1940s pleased the shippers who received them because they were in good condition for loading and could carry more freight than the cars they replaced; as Scribbins notes in *The Milwaukee Road 1928–1985*, one group of cars turned out by the shops that year represented "the largest capacity steel box cars in the United States and probably in the world."

In a special report covering the period December 1, 1945, through August 31, 1950 (roughly the first five years after emerging from its second bankruptcy), Milwaukee management said it had acquired or ordered a total of 15,496 freight cars, at a cost of $53.2 million. The Milwaukee Road closed out the 1940s with an equipment fleet consisting of:

- 1,144 locomotives including 910 steam, 185 diesel, and 49 electric;
- 58,714 freight cars, including 25,686 boxcars, 11,482 gondolas, 6,390 automobile cars, 4,296 hoppers, 3,746 stock cars, and 7,114 other types including flat, ore, and ballast cars;

In both steam and diesel days, the Milwaukee roster included engines whose axle loadings suited them for service on branchlines with weight restrictions. In April 1972, these six-axle Alco road switchers (RSC2s 596 and 594 and RSD5 572) were based at La Crosse for use on the Viroqua Branch, but on this day they are on the mainline, en route westbound on the Lisbon Patrol, at Camp Douglas, Wisconsin. *Bob Anderson*

- 808 cabooses;
- 1,086 passenger cars, including 446 express and mail cars, 386 coaches, 87 sleepers, 70 combination baggage and passenger cars, 48 diners, 43 parlor and parlor-café cars, and 6 "tap" (lounge) cars;
- 2 rail motor cars; and
- 1 tugboat and 4 car barges (for service between Seattle/Tacoma and the Olympic Peninsula).

Even though diesels represented a minority of the railroad's locomotive fleet, they were beginning to have a big impact. As recently as 1945, only 13 percent of the company's ton-miles and 9 percent of its passenger car-miles were generated by diesel power. In 1949, with diesels constituting 16 percent of the motive-power fleet, they handled 51 percent of the company's passenger business, 45 percent of its yard switching, and 29 percent of its road freight service.

Over the next two years, as the diesel fleet grew rapidly, there would be a dramatic change in the way Milwaukee powered its trains. By 1951, diesels performed 86 percent of the railroad's passenger service, 76 percent of its road freight operations, and 74 percent of its yard switching.

In its annual report for 1954, written in early 1955, management declared, "the motive power of the company is now 100% dieselized and electrified, making The Milwaukee Road the first one in the Northwest to be so operated." Scribbins reports that "S2 4-8-4 #239 handled Way Freight 91 from La Crosse, Wisconsin, to St. Paul," on January 4, 1955, marking the end of regularly scheduled steam service on the Milwaukee.

There would continue to be irregular use of steam power for the next couple of years, however. The final steam operation on the railroad, Scribbins says, "was that of Class G8 4-6-0 #1004 on the night of March 15–16,

Although the 600-horsepower SW1 was used as a switch engine on most railroads, on the Milwaukee its light axle loadings made it ideal for operation on lines such as the Caledonia branch in southern Minnesota, where bridges would not support heavier power. Here, SW1 860, built in 1940, leads three identical units at Preston in February 1976. *Steve Glischinski*

1957 when it made a roundtrip between Austin, Minnesota and La Crosse, Wisconsin, on passenger trains 158 and 157," acting as substitute power for the trains' usual motorcar. The 1004 illustrated the longevity of steam locomotives: it was originally constructed in 1901, and rebuilt in 1920.

Yards also began to get attention in the years following the war. Terminal operations are a critical factor in the survival of any railroad because they affect costs, service quality, and the ability to maintain fluid operations during heavy traffic periods. As diesel power began to replace steam, longer trains were possible, which meant that important yards needed to be reconfigured to handle them.

In 1951, the railroad upgraded Air Line Yard in Milwaukee. This was a key facility on the Milwaukee not just because of the business generated by local industries but because traffic from most of Wisconsin, Michigan, Minnesota, and points west flowed through Milwaukee en route to customers and connecting lines in Chicago. Scribbins writes that the upgrading of the Air Line hump yard, which began in 1951 and continued the following year, increased its switching capacity "from 350–400 cars to more than 800 per shift. . . . The retarders were the first on any railroad to feature speed controls enabling a car to coast through the yard at speeds determined by the control tower operator."

The next major yard project was at Bensenville, Illinois, 17 miles west of the Chicago Loop. Here, a $5.5 million project produced a yard with 33 westbound classification tracks, 37 eastbound classification and departure tracks, 5 tracks for departing westbound trains, 20 receiving tracks, and a total standing capacity in these 95 tracks of 7,497 cars. Both eastbound and westbound classification tracks were fed by having cars shoved over a single hump; operators in two retarder towers then controlled the speed of cars into

103

Milwaukee RS3 road switcher 453 has a pair of trucks from an Alco switch engine, in this view at the joint Milwaukee–Kansas City Southern yard in Kansas City in May 1966. *Steve Patterson*

the yard tracks. Design switching capacity of the yard was 3,600 cars per 24-hour day. One Milwaukee veteran who worked at Bensenville in the mid-1960s reports that on a regular basis the yard switched between 2,600 and 2,800 cars daily.

The third major yard in the Chicago–Twin Cities corridor was also the beneficiary of an upgrading project. Starting in 1955, the railroad spent $5 million to expand and upgrade its St. Paul Yard. Work was completed in 1956; the rebuilt yard had 35 classification tracks with a standing capacity of 1,692 cars, plus seven receiving and six departure tracks. Until Burlington Northern built its Northtown Yard in Minneapolis in the 1970s, the Milwaukee facility was the only hump yard in the Twin Cities.

In the postwar years, the Milwaukee also invested in new signaling equipment to improve safety, speed the movement of trains over the road, and reduce the costs associated with having operators located at stations to deliver train orders to crews. In its 1955 edition, *Moody's Transportation Manual* reported that at the end of 1954, the company had 740 miles of road covered by Centralized Traffic Control and "2,911 miles of Controlled Automatic Block Signals, which is equivalent to C.T.C., except switches are not electrically operated."

Financial and Competitive Realities

The postwar era was one of renewal and revitalization for the railroad industry. The diesel locomotive eliminated many maintenance functions at terminals, enabled trains to run through intermediate points with only a brief stop, and eliminated the railroads' dependence on coal as a fuel. Other technological changes, including CTC, the use of data processing in both headquarters and line-operating functions, and the mechanization of track maintenance, had beneficial

The Milwaukee's flagship electric motive power from 1951 until the end of electrified operations in 1974 was the group of 12 streamlined, double-ended units commonly known as "Little Joes." Originally designed for the Soviet Union's state railways but never delivered there, the locomotives derived their name from dictator Joseph Stalin. Assigned exclusively to the Rocky Mountain Division between Avery, Idaho, and Harlowton, Montana, the Joes were equipped to operate in multiple with diesels. This eastbound freight is preparing to depart Avery with Joes E77 and E75 and GP9 321 in September 1972. *Phil Mason*

In this circa-1950 photo, Class F6 Hudsons 132 and 131 share the Avery, Idaho, engine terminal with boxcab E34 and a Little Joe. *Photo by Philip Hastings, courtesy of California State Railroad Museum/negative no. 3127*

impacts on railroad income statements and on the quality of service to the customer.

But while the railroads were becoming more efficient in their operations, the competitive landscape was changing. In 1954, after almost 20 years of talk about a new federally subsidized highway system, President Eisenhower endorsed the concept. It took two more years to turn the idea into legislation, and in 1956 the Federal Highway Act gave birth to the Interstate System. Even without the interstates, trucks had been eating away at the railroads' market share, and automobiles had replaced the passenger train for much personal travel. Meanwhile, the airline industry was also benefiting from technological improvements, and from federal willingness to subsidize airport construction. Over the next few years, the airlines would take from the railroads another longtime source of revenue: the U.S. Mail.

The Milwaukee faced a greater disparity between costs and revenues than most railroads. As management had said in the company's 1948 annual report, "the physical aspects of the railroad are not conducive to low cost operation... with its far flung property, relatively low traffic density and high terminal and station expenses."

The problem of low traffic density, which translated into low returns on invested capital, would bedevil the Milwaukee for the remaining years of its life. The Milwaukee had to compete for capital with companies that offered greater return on investment. The result: for the last several decades of its existence, there was never enough money for new cars, new locomotives, new rail, or the other physical assets needed to sustain a railroad.

In a different regulatory environment, with greater pricing freedoms and fewer

Above: A westbound freight passes the Three Forks, Montana, depot, powered by two Little Joes and three GP9s, circa 1960. *Milwaukee Road photo, author collection* Left: This is what a westbound train at Three Forks looked like in 1979, with the wires gone. *Phil Mason*

The Little Joes had been in service a little more than a year when they appeared in this March 1952 ad to promote the company's freight service. *Author collection*

barriers to exiting markets (and lines) that were not paying their way, the Milwaukee might have survived. However, this was not the reality of the early 1950s. The Milwaukee might have been a privately owned, for-profit business, but the rules under which it operated, as written by congress and administered by the Interstate Commerce Commission, were those of a public utility.

The difficulty of eliminating light-density lines was illustrated by the fact that in the five years from 1946 through 1950, only two lines were abandoned: a 47.5-mile segment between DeKalb and Joliet, Illinois (22.5 miles of which comprised trackage rights over Elgin, Joliet & Eastern); and a 13.7-mile line between Reno and Caledonia, Minnesota, most of which was washed out as a result of flooding.

Two of the Milwaukee's 12 Little Joes, E20 and E21, were initially assigned to passenger service. These two units were equipped with boilers to provide steam for heat. They remained in passenger service until 1958. In October 1972 they are at the head end of an eastbound train east of Haugan, Montana. *Tom Murray*

Mounting labor costs were also taking their toll on the Milwaukee. Proportionally, the impact on the company's operating expenses may have been no more serious than on other railroads, but given its thin financial margins, the effect on the Milwaukee's bottom line was greater. These costs related not only to a series of postwar wage increases, but also to such changes as paid vacations (implemented in 1941), the 40-hour week (begun in 1949), and mandatory retirement and pensions for nonunion employees. By becoming more efficient through a combination of technology and more cost-effective operating practices, the Milwaukee was able to reduce its overall employment from 38,268 in 1948 to 27,961 in 1954. But because of inflation in labor costs, this 27 percent reduction in staffing was accompanied by a drop of less than 9 percent in compensation.

The company's freight business took a big hit in 1954 as the U.S. economy went into recession. Freight revenues, which stood at $215.4 million in 1953, dropped 8.3 percent, to $197.5 million. They improved a bit in 1955 but remained well below the levels of the 1951–1953 period.

Against this background of competitive and financial challenges, the Milwaukee's decision to consider a possible merger with rival Chicago & North Western, beginning in late 1954, is understandable. In fact, the two midwestern roads were not alone in looking at ways to save money by merging or coordinating their operations. Shortly before the Milwaukee and C&NW made their announcement, the Louisville & Nashville and Nashville, Chattanooga & St. Louis had agreed to merge; their union would be consummated in 1957. Early in 1955, the Erie and the Lackawanna implemented a coordination plan, and there was talk from executives of both the New Haven and the Delaware & Hudson about possible mergers in the northeast.

Historian Richard Saunders says these developments may have been coincidental, but "the time was right" in view of the dropoff in rail traffic following the end of the Korean conflict and the recession of 1954. None of the northeastern mergers would come to pass in the near term, but it was clear that railroad executives were thinking and talking among themselves about the benefits of coordination and consolidation.

The Milwaukee–C&NW merger idea would be dropped, too, as management of both companies backed away from the idea, but it was not dead.

In 1956, another merger proposal was announced that would be of great interest to the Milwaukee's owners, employees, and customers. Great Northern and Northern Pacific, and their jointly owned subsidiaries — Chicago, Burlington & Quincy and Spokane, Portland & Seattle—announced that they were studying consolidation. It would be 14 years, however, until the Burlington Northern merger took place, as regulators and courts grappled with the economic and competitive issues associated with such an unprecedented rail consolidation. For the next several years, it seemed that one merger proposal or another was always on the table, involving either the Milwaukee or its neighbors. The Milwaukee was on notice that the landscape was not stable, and that one of its future roles might be to serve as the principal rail competitor to a unified Northern Lines in the Northwest.

Services To Meet the Needs of the Marketplace

At the end of 1957, John Kiley retired as president of The Milwaukee Road. William J. Quinn succeeded him on January 1, 1958. At age 46, Quinn was younger than either Kiley or Charles Buford had been when appointed president. While they had come from the operating and engineering side of the business, and were longtime Milwaukee Road employees, Quinn was a lawyer whose résumé included stints as a district attorney and FBI agent. Prior to joining the law department of The Milwaukee Road in April 1954, he was vice president of law at the Minneapolis, St. Paul & Sault Ste. Marie (commonly known as the Soo Line).

Quinn had only been in the president's office a short time when the Minneapolis & St. Louis broached the idea of merger with the Milwaukee. However, the idea did not progress, and M&StL instead was acquired by C&NW. Another abortive merger proposal involved the Milwaukee and the Chicago, Rock Island & Pacific. This one first surfaced in 1959, but it, too, was shelved after being studied by both railroads.

During Quinn's tenure, the Milwaukee responded to highway competition by offering various nontraditional services. Trailer-on-flatcar (TOFC) service, or piggyback, was already well established in the rail industry by the late 1950s, but the Milwaukee was looking for something extra that would give it a competitive advantage. It thought it had found the answer in early 1959 when it became the second major railroad (after New York Central) to introduce Flexi-Van service. The Flexi-Van was a forerunner of today's intermodal container. It traveled by rail on a specially equipped flatcar, and when it reached its destination it was transferred to a highway bogie for over-the-road movement. By not transporting the highway wheels between rail terminals, Flexi-Van service reduced dead weight and enjoyed a lower center of gravity than TOFC shipments.

The Milwaukee initially seemed pleased with customers' acceptance of Flexi-Van technology. The annual report for 1959 described success stories including shipments by an online meat packer, transoceanic movements from Japan (without transloading), and mail distribution by the postal service. However, Flexi-Van never reached critical mass. There would often be too many vans at a terminal for the available bogies, or vice versa. Only Milwaukee, New York Central, and Illinois Central adopted the system; over the next ten years it withered and eventually disappeared.

At the same time, the Milwaukee experimented with what it described as "the country's first transcontinental piggybacking of automobiles." Cars were shipped by highway from Michigan assembly plants to Chicago,

Above: A quiet night at Avery, Idaho, in the mid-1960s finds a trio of Little Joes between runs. *Don Sims*
Left: Milwaukee Little Joe E21 at Alberton, Montana, in June 1973. *Stan Smaill*

Milwaukee-originated iron ore was originally forwarded to Escanaba via the Escanaba & Lake Superior Railroad, but in later years the Chicago & North Western performed this function. In January 1973, the Milwaukee's Groveland Mine run has exchanged cars with C&NW's Antoine Turn, and is at Iron Mountain, Michigan, headed back to the mine with empties. The train is passing over the C&NW line to Iron River and Ironwood. *Bob Anderson*

where they were transferred to specially built piggyback trailers and then forwarded on Milwaukee Road trains to either Miles City, Montana, or Spokane. The experiment, says Scribbins, lasted about two years. Multilevel auto racks replaced the piggyback concept; they allowed an all-rail movement, eliminating the need for transloading at Chicago.

Both TOFC and multilevels were higher than conventional railcars, posing a problem for the Milwaukee, as it did for many other railroads. The Milwaukee had to lower the floor of its one Wisconsin tunnel, near Tomah, by 26 inches to accommodate both multilevels and standard-height TOFC trailers. In 1961 and 1962, similar work was done on 31 tunnels on Lines West.

Former passenger engines E21 and E20 show off the unmistakable Little Joe profile near Sappington, Montana, in August 1973. **Steve Patterson**

In 1963, the Milwaukee added new, expedited train service between Chicago and the Pacific Northwest (train 261, the *XL Special*, and 262, the *Thunderhawk*). It followed this with a marketing blitz by employees in special red vests and neckties.

Unit trains for coal and grain were also implemented in the 1960s, improving both operating costs and equipment productivity, and at the same time making service more predictable than with single-car or multi-car shipments handled on conventional freight trains. Although both operations were limited in scope (the coal trains ran from Indiana mines to an Indiana utility, and the grain trains were seasonal), they demonstrated the economic and service benefits of unit-train service.

During much of the 1960s, Milwaukee Shops were kept busy upgrading and rebuilding the railroad's freight-car fleet. The annual report for 1964 described a repair program begun in 1963 that produced 5,300

Train 369 is northbound in August 1972 at Iron Mountain, Michigan. Four extra GP30 units power the train en route to Hanna Mining Company's Groveland Mine, where they will be used to power an ore train destined for Granite City, Illinois. Such all-rail iron ore moves were unusual; most of the Milwaukee's ore traffic was transloaded to Great Lakes vessels at Escanaba, Michigan. *Bob Anderson*

cars "put into like-new condition for revenue service." Another 1,200 cars were lengthened or otherwise rebuilt for greater freight-hauling capacity. Old 40-foot boxcars were stretched to the more marketable 50-foot length, and given "DF2" markings to indicate that they were equipped to keep freight "damage free."

In 1966, new all-TOFC trains 98 and 99 were established between Chicago and the Twin Cities on overnight schedules. This move was aimed directly at truckers, which dominated the movement of manufactured goods in this corridor.

Throughout the 1960s, the Milwaukee had been expanding its use of computers to improve its revenue and car-accounting functions; to provide operational, sales, and marketing support; and to provide timely car location information to customers. The railroad's Carscope system, implemented in 1959, was continually enhanced to provide more efficient and accurate processing and distribution of information about car locations, pickups, setouts, and interchanges.

But the problem that the railroad's management had put its finger on in 1949—the fact that the Milwaukee was a "relatively low traffic density" carrier—had not changed significantly in the intervening years. In 1966, according to *Moody's Transportation Manual*, the Milwaukee had a revenue freight density (i.e., tons of freight carried by the railroad, divided by total system mileage) of 1.59 million. Even C&NW, which, like the Milwaukee, was burdened with thousands of miles of branchlines, was a little better, at 1.64 million. Most worrisome was that the major components of the soon-to-be-merged

Above: In October 1973, the Groveland Mine run with four EMD units—two F7s and two GP9s—is at Randville, Michigan, en route to the mine to spot empties. *Bob Anderson* Left: Pulpwood was a big commodity in northern Wisconsin and on the Upper Peninsula of Michigan. Here, two Fairbanks-Morse H16-44 units, 423 and 424, pick up loads at Sidnaw, Michigan, in August 1964. *Steve Patterson*

Fairbanks-Morse–built locomotives at Beloit, Wisconsin, on the Milwaukee's Racine & Southwestern Division. Milwaukee 526 and 529 were part of a group of six Fairbanks-Morse H16-66 locomotives acquired by the railroad in 1953. Here, they pull a cut of cars out of St. Paul Yard past the Hoffman Avenue interlocking tower in January 1974. *Tom Murray*

Northern Lines had significantly greater traffic density. NP's was 2.12 million, GN's was 2.34 million, and CB&Q's was 2.41 million.

In addition, despite the fact that during the 1950s and 1960s price inflation was a fact of life, over time the Milwaukee got less, not more, out of each ton that it hauled. In 1958, it brought in 1.48 cents for every ton-mile it generated; by 1966, that number had fallen to 1.31 cents. This problem, like the density issue, was not unique to the Milwaukee, but the decline in revenue yield could not go on forever.

The question that the Milwaukee faced during the 1960s was whether all of its marketing campaigns, service improvements, cost-saving initiatives, and investments in facilities and equipment would be enough, in the aggregate, to allow it to survive as an independent company.

Below: Beginning in 1969 and continuing into the early 1970s, Milwaukee Shops upgraded more than 50 of the railroad's GP9s to what the railroad called a "GP20," though they were more accurately described as "GP20m" units. MILW 999, shown here at St. Paul in October 1977, was the first such unit to be modified.
Steve Glischinski

Mergers and the Milwaukee

The next major merger proposal involving the Milwaukee was a revival in 1966 of the Milwaukee–C&NW plan, which followed several years of discussion between the companies. Unlike the M&StL and CRI&P merger studies, this one was actually submitted to shareholders and to the ICC for approval.

In October 1966 Quinn left the Milwaukee to become president of the CB&Q. This was at a time when the GN–NP–CB&Q–SP&S merger proposal was making its way through the regulatory process. The ICC's decision in this case would have profound implications for The Milwaukee Road.

Curtiss E. Crippen, who was 58 when he became president, and whose background resembled those of Buford and Kiley more than Quinn's, succeeded Quinn . He had been with The Milwaukee Road since 1930, and had served in both the engineering and operating departments before becoming vice president of finance and accounting in 1961.

Strategically, one of Crippen's top priorities was to complete the merger with C&NW, which would allow cost savings through consolidation of parallel lines and duplicate facilities, and create a stronger competitor vis-à-vis the large western railroads. However, at this time there was no deadline for the ICC to rule on a merger proposal. Hearings lasted almost a year. An ICC examiner recommended approval in December 1968, but it was not the final word.

While the Milwaukee–C&NW merger application was working its way through the ICC's regulatory machinery, the North Western's stock price had dropped to a fraction of its previous value. The ICC ruled in early 1970 that the merger agreement's stock exchange ratio should be revisited. Soon afterward, C&NW's parent company, Northwest Industries, canceled the stock exchange and instead offered to sell its railroad to the Milwaukee. The Milwaukee chose not to pursue such a transaction, and the merger died.

The Milwaukee remained optimistic, however, that the Northern Lines merger, which it had initially opposed, would help rectify the density problem, and be an important ingredient in the Milwaukee's own survival formula. The Milwaukee had said that it would support the Northerns' merger provided that it received specific commercial concessions, which would give it the ability to compete for traffic long unavailable to it because of routing restrictions and other barriers. The Milwaukee's conditions included:

- Opening of 11 interchange points in Washington, Montana, and North Dakota between the Milwaukee and the newly merged railroad;
- Access to Portland, Oregon;
- Trackage rights north of Seattle, to allow the Milwaukee to tap into Canadian traffic and exit its own deteriorated Cedar Falls–Monroe Line; and
- Access to Billings, Montana, through a car haulage agreement.

On February 2, 1970, the U.S. Supreme Court ruled in favor of the Great Northern Pacific & Burlington Lines merger, which would be implemented under the simpler corporate title "Burlington Northern." The world in which The Milwaukee Road operated was about to change. The Milwaukee Road's 1969 annual report, issued in early 1970, said that the Supreme Court's action was "welcome news," because of the new traffic that the Milwaukee could now compete for. Whether the Milwaukee was in any condition to handle that traffic was an open question.

A Financial Tipping Point

The Milwaukee had made money during the late 1950s and most of the 1960s—not a lot, but enough to keep its head above water. According to *Moody's Transportation Manual*, in the ten years through 1967, Milwaukee's income before fixed charges averaged 1.46 times its financial obligations. This was better

The Milwaukee assigned most of its General Electric locomotives to Lines West. Here, U25B 391 and U28B 397 are part of a set of four units on the head end of a westbound freight setting out cars at Plummer, Idaho, in the mid-1960s. *Don Sims*

than Rock Island (1.32), on a par with C&NW (1.48), but well below NP (3.03), CB&Q (3.24), and GN (4.22).

One difference between a railroad making a lot of money and one that scrapes by is that the latter has a slimmer margin of safety to weather downturns in traffic. That's exactly what happened to The Milwaukee Road in 1969, when a nationwide economic slowdown and severe winter weather (followed by spring floods) conspired to eliminate its margin of financial safety. The company ended the year with a net loss of $5.6 million, as opposed to net income of $6 million in 1968. The loss widened to $8.9 million in 1970.

These losses marked a tipping point in the fortunes of The Milwaukee Road. The railroad was not suddenly transformed from a moneymaker to a money-loser. The process was much more gradual than that. In fact, there would be bright spots in the coming years, when it appeared that the Milwaukee might actually have a future as an independent, self-sustaining railroad. But the financial losses of 1969 and 1970 indicated that the railroad had begun to lose its resilience, its ability to withstand adversity.

In July 1973, a group of 3,000-horsepower SD40-2 units was delivered to the Milwaukee for use on Lines West. They carried Locotrol equipment that permitted radio-controlled helper operations. Prior to being sent west, MILW 27 (a Locotrol "slave") and 25 (a Locotrol "master") are on a shakedown run at Kingsford, Michigan. *Bob Anderson*

CHAPTER SEVEN

THE FINAL YEARS:
1970–1985

The Milwaukee Road's life as a corporate entity ended in 1985, when Soo Line Railroad Company absorbed its rail operating assets. But it did not go quietly. It was not taken over by a federally supported corporation, as several bankrupt northeastern railroads were when Conrail was created in 1976. Nor did it simply cease operations, as the Rock Island did in 1980.

Throughout the period from 1970 to 1985, those responsible for the operation of The Milwaukee Road tried to make it successful.

121

The creation of Amtrak in April 1971 brought about many changes to service and equipment assignments. One innovation was through service between Milwaukee and St. Louis, operated as the *Prairie State* and the *Abraham Lincoln*, which ran from November 14, 1971, until October 1, 1973. This was the only time that Chicago served as an intermediate stop rather than the origin or destination of a passenger train. Train 301, the *Prairie State*, is shown at Joliet, Illinois, in December 1971, operating on the Illinois Central Gulf, with ex-Milwaukee Road power and cars of former Burlington, Milwaukee, Atlantic Coast Line, Union Pacific, and Gulf, Mobile & Ohio ownership. *Phil Gosney*

Different stakeholders in the railroad often had differing views of what "success" was, but when the dust settled, most of the freight that had once moved over the Milwaukee was still able to move via rail; the company's debts had been paid off; and a substantial number of its employees continued to work in the rail industry.

Milwaukee Road Passenger Service Comes to an End

The Milwaukee Road had a proud tradition of passenger train operation, but by 1970 it was well past the point where the financial burden of carrying on this tradition made sense. When the *Olympian Hiawatha* was discontinued as a Chicago–Seattle train in 1961, it was symbolic of the fact that the world had changed: long-distance passenger trains, whatever social benefits they produced, could not be operated at a profit in the age of the jet airliner and interstate highways. This situation wasn't unique to The Milwaukee Road. Throughout the rail industry there was pressure for a publicly funded solution to the passenger train issue.

The problem was solved, or at least transferred to the federal government, in 1971, with the formation of Amtrak. Upon payment of certain fees, the freight railroads would be able to transfer their intercity passenger services to Amtrak. Henceforth, if a railroad's routes were part of the Amtrak network, it would operate trains on a contract basis, and would not be liable for the operating expenses associated with those trains.

The Milwaukee chose to join Amtrak, and its Chicago–Twin Cities route once again began to host trains to and from the Pacific Northwest: *The Empire Builder* service, which operated via Burlington Northern west of the Twin Cities. (There was some irony in this,

Two Little Joes and a three-unit boxcab set lead an eastbound freight across the Clark Fork River at St. Regis, Montana, in June 1973. The boxcabs are en route, dead in tow, to the shop at Deer Lodge. *Stan Smaill*

Below: These units, led by MILW 119A, have just uncoupled from their train after arriving at the Milwaukee's South Minneapolis Yard from St. Paul in August 1977. *Steve Glischinski*

Above: Little Joes E72 and E79 arrive at Avery, Idaho, in August 1973, with a westbound train, which will be forwarded by a three-unit set of diesels. *Steve Patterson* Right: A trio of Milwaukee F-units leads a train over the Indiana Harbor Belt (IHB) at McCook, Illinois, in September 1974. The Milwaukee was 49 percent owner of the IHB, with majority ownership in the hands of New York Central (and successors Penn Central and Conrail). Today, ownership of IHB is split among Canadian Pacific, CSX, and Norfolk Southern. *Tom Murray*

since the name of the train referred to Great Northern founder James J. Hill, who had a profound and not necessarily beneficial influence on The Milwaukee Road.) Additional service would operate between Milwaukee and Chicago. In 1971 the Milwaukee reported a special charge of $24.2 million as the cost of entering Amtrak and thereby exiting the intercity passenger business. Much of this charge related to a write-off of passenger facilities that the company would no longer need.

This still left the Milwaukee with its Chicago-area suburban passenger operations: the North Line to Fox Lake and the West Line to Elgin. By the early 1970s, in both Chicago and other cities with intensive rail commuter operations, there was a recognition that public funding of such operations was the only practical way to ensure that they survived. On the Milwaukee, such funding began in the early 1970s with capital grants to support the Elgin service. These grants, from the state and federal governments, were channeled through the Northwest Suburban Mass Transit District. Two parallel organizations, the North Suburban and Greater Lake County Mass Transit Districts, came into existence to support the Fox Lake service and other local transit operations.

With the formation of the Regional Transportation Authority (RTA) in 1974, embracing five northeastern Illinois counties, a vehicle now existed through which the Milwaukee could receive operating subsidies, as well as capital funding, for its suburban service. In 1975 the Milwaukee and RTA signed a purchase-of-service agreement that substantially relieved the railroad of its financial responsibility for the service. That was not the end of the uncertainty over suburban service funding, however; RTA had financial problems in 1981 that threatened to end its payments to the Milwaukee and, indirectly, bring an end to the service itself. However, the 1982 formation of a new entity,

Northwest Suburban Mass Transit District No. 47, carrying the name of on-line community River Grove, Illinois, pushes train 128 toward Chicago in August 1974, as it clatters over the Elgin, Joliet & Eastern diamond at Rondout. *Tom Murray*

Right: Milwaukee SD40-2s 3007 and 180 prepare to depart the St. Paul intermodal facility with a piggyback train for Chicago in December 1973. *Tom Murray*
Below: The Milwaukee received ten GP38-2s (Nos. 356–365) from EMD in September 1974. Soon after being delivered, Milwaukee 361 and another GP38-2 are at the Bensenville, Illinois, engine house. *Don Sims*

Northeastern Illinois Railroad Company (NIRC), under RTA, to operate all Chicago-area commuter service got The Milwaukee Road out of the passenger train business completely and ensured the continued operation of service on the North and West lines. Today, NIRC is known as Metra, and the two lines continue in operation as the Metra Milwaukee District.

The other significant event of 1971 was a decision to form a holding company, Chicago Milwaukee Corporation (CMC), which would be able to branch out into non-transportation businesses. The holding company came into existence in January 1972. It's not clear how much of the motivation for this idea came from a genuine desire to protect shareholders against the cyclical financial results of the transportation business, and how much of it came from a desire to find profitable businesses whose income could be sheltered by tax benefits carried over from the years when The Milwaukee Road lost money. But it was a fashionable thing to do in the railroad industry, and The Milwaukee Road's management apparently saw merit in the idea even if CMC's non-railroad businesses never really amounted to much.

In 1973 and 1974, the railroad produced net income of $12.8 million and $11.4 million, respectively. They would be the last years of positive net income for The Milwaukee Road. As management explained to shareholders, the year 1975 produced "manifestly unsatisfactory" results. The economy was in recession, and in the Milwaukee's view there were "simply too many railroads competing for what business the western United States has to offer railroads, clearly too much duplication of rail service and rail facilities."

In early 1977, after another year of red ink on the bottom line, the company told shareholders, "revenues were insufficient to cover the cost of operating a railroad plant

Former passenger engine FP45 leads an eastbound freight waiting for a signal to enter Bensenville Yard on April 1975. On the head end of the train are several cars of auto frames produced at A. O. Smith in Milwaukee, to be interchanged to eastern railroads at Chicago for delivery to auto assembly plants. *Tom Murray*

127

In 1971, the Milwaukee gained access to Portland, Oregon, as a condition of the Burlington Northern merger. In August 1972, General Electric U30B MILW 6002 leads a southbound train en route to Portland past BN's Vancouver, Washington, station. *Phil Mason*

with too much capacity for the markets it serves." The situation could not continue.

The U.S. Rail Map Changes

On March 2, 1970, Burlington Northern began its existence as a corporate entity. The Milwaukee would now be able to compete for traffic at 11 interchange points formerly closed to it. However, what the Milwaukee called "the most meaningful" of the ICC-imposed conditions—its entry to Portland, Oregon—was delayed until March 22, 1971. Once it arrived in Portland, the Milwaukee could compete for transcontinental traffic handled in conjunction with a friendly connecting line there (Southern Pacific). It could also go after north-south traffic between Portland and Sumas, Washington, where it interchanged with Canadian roads.

Following a decade of modest financial returns and resulting deferred maintenance, much of the Milwaukee's physical plant was not up to task of handling more traffic. Renewal of rails and ties had not kept pace with the rest of the industry; in fact, says one company veteran, its maintenance program was "grossly inadequate." Slow orders were common, not just on branchlines, but on the mainline as well.

The Portland extension put substantial volumes of new business on the railroad. In March 1971, operation of trains 261 (*XL Special*) and 262 (*Thunderhawk*) was extended beyond Tacoma to Portland, and by June of that year, a third pair of trains had been added to the western extension. Scribbins notes that this was "the first time three freights were scheduled in each direction" between Tacoma and St. Paul.

However, the Milwaukee would have preferred not simply the conditions it got from the BN merger, but to be part of BN. In 1973, it asked the ICC to include it in the merged company, and for a time Milwaukee and BN officials met to discuss such a possibility. But BN broke off the talks in 1974 and the ICC finally said no in 1976. Some at the Milwaukee felt that BN had deliberately taken actions to undermine the value of the merger conditions. Such allegations, described by former Milwaukee attorney Tom Ploss in his book, *The Nation Pays Again*, were never tested in any legal venue, but they left a legacy of bad feeling among some Lines West employees.

The Milwaukee was determined to get the most possible benefit out of other railroads' mergers. It wasn't playing the role of a spoiler. The Milwaukee could legitimately make the case that as its connecting lines and competitors merged, it faced the real possibility of losing traffic and having its financial

When trackwork or derailments necessitated a detour in Montana, the parallel NP route provided a handy alternative. On this day in August 1973, a Milwaukee train led by SD40-2 3037 is on Burlington Northern (ex-NP) trackage at Dixon, Montana. *Steve Patterson*

condition made worse, unless it could gain some offsetting advantage.

Besides BN, the other merger case where the Milwaukee came away with what it considered a valuable condition involved the Louisville & Nashville and the Monon. In approving this merger, the ICC granted the Milwaukee trackage rights to Louisville, where it would have a new friendly connection for traffic to and from the Southeast: Southern Railway. The L&N mounted a legal challenge to the Milwaukee's entry to Louisville, but on

The Milwaukee Road's Michigan iron ore operations overlapped to a large degree with those of Chicago & North Western. It's August of 1977, and according to the photographer's notes, "the Milwaukee's Mine Run out of Channing has just delivered 95 loads of Groveland pellets to the C&NW's Antoine yard in Iron Mountain, Michigan. The crew is getting a bite to eat as the C&NW's Antoine Turn out of Escanaba arrives early in the afternoon with the empties. After the C&NW yards the empties, the Milwaukee crew will place their caboose on the tail end, run the units around to the west end of the train, shove out of the yard and head for Groveland Mine. After spotting the empties at the mine they will return caboose hop to Channing." *Mike Cleary*

The northbound Louisville–Bensenville train, near Orleans, Indiana, on Louisville & Nashville (ex-Monon) trackage with a quintet of GP20 units in May 1979. The first car is one of the Milwaukee's 100-ton-capacity covered hoppers (weighing 263,000 pounds fully loaded). This car type became more common in the rail industry throughout the 1970s, although it meant the death knell for some of the Milwaukee's branchlines that could only handle cars up to 220,000 pounds in weight. *Dave Gayer*

March 1, 1973, the first Milwaukee Road train entered the Kentucky city.

One intriguing might-have-been from the early 1970s relates to a conversation that reportedly took place between C&NW's Ben Heineman and Milwaukee Chairman William Quinn, soon after the latter returned to The Milwaukee Road in early 1970. After the ICC had said that the stock exchange ratio in the proposed Milwaukee–C&NW merger should be renegotiated, C&NW's parent company, Northwest Industries, dropped the merger idea and made it clear that it wanted to sell the railroad. Ploss reports that Heineman approached Quinn to discuss specific terms under which such a transaction might take place, but Quinn rebuffed the C&NW's efforts.

The Puget Sound Extension: Decline and Exit

The BN merger conditions, particularly entry to Portland, had generated substantial business for The Milwaukee Road. However, it lacked the financial resources necessary to bring the western extension up to a condition that would support three trains a day in each direction.

The first symbolic act in The Milwaukee Road's exit from the West came in February 1973, when the railroad said it would end its electrified operations. Internally, some Milwaukee Road managers had argued for the electrification to be modernized, rather than scrapped, but the cost of doing so was deemed too high. A special

Next page: Train 201 heads west out of Three Forks, Montana, on May 31, 1979. Phil Mason

Below: Milwaukee electric switcher E81 (originally numbered 10051), shown here at Deer Lodge, Montana, was built in 1916, one of a pair of switchers that were the first electric locomotives to see service on the CM&StP's Puget Sound extension. Don Sims

supplement to the railroad's employee magazine explained the decision this way:

> Advances in diesel locomotives have negated many of the onetime advantages of electrified operation. Use of electric locomotives on the Rocky Mountain Division has for several years been limited to helper, booster and yard service. No electrically powered trains have moved on the Coast Division since 1971. Electric operations on the Rocky Mountain Division accounted for about 19 percent of the locomotive miles operated on that division in 1972. Only three percent of the total locomotive miles operated on the entire Milwaukee Road system in 1972 were electrically operated. Viewed in this context, the announcement of the decision to phase-out the electrification was not a major change in policy, but was rather official acknowledgment of the inevitability of existing operational realities.

The timing couldn't have been worse in terms of the economic tradeoff between electrified and diesel operations, since the price of diesel fuel would soon skyrocket as a result of an embargo by oil-producing countries. Nevertheless, the last electrified operation would take place in June 1974 at Deer Lodge. Scribbins notes, "Milwaukee electrifi-

One victim of The Milwaukee Road's retrenchment during its final years was the Council Bluffs Line, but in 1978, the line was still controlled by Milwaukee Road train dispatchers at Perry, Iowa. The portion of the control panel (or "model board" in railroad parlance) shown here covers the territory between West Perry and Melbourne, Iowa. *John Leopard*

cation ended the same way it had started more than 58 years earlier, using a General Electric steeple-cab goat."

If the decision to cease electric operations was controversial, the efforts by trustee Stanley Hillman and his successor, Richard Ogilvie, to completely terminate operations on the Puget Sound extension was even more so. Hillman and Ogilvie believed that if The Milwaukee Road was to emerge from bankruptcy, it could only do so by paring back to a "core" operation, consisting of the routes in the Upper Midwest. Dissenters, most notably, employees on Lines West who would face the loss of their employment, believed that a profitable railroad could be built around the routes west of the Twin Cities. This belief led to the formation of the Association to Save Our Railroad Employment (SORE), which did an analysis demonstrating, it said, the potential profitability of Lines West.

The sticking point in any economic analysis of Lines West was the cost of rehabilitating the physical plant. One former Milwaukee executive says that management estimated this cost at between $120 and $140 million. The railroad did not have the resources to fund a capital expenditure of this magnitude, and there were no obvious external sources of capital to do the job. The SORE initiative failed to win support from the trustee, from the Milwaukee's bankruptcy court, or from the Interstate Commerce Commission.

The controversy played out from August 1978, when trustee Hillman announced his belief that the western extension should not be part of a reorganized Milwaukee Road, until February 1980, when the embargo of many route-miles in the Dakotas, western Montana, Idaho, and Washington took place. Since other railroads accessed many of the traffic-generating locations along the route, the abandonment of major segments of the Puget Sound extension still left most shippers with rail service. In March 1981, BN purchased several pieces of the former Milwaukee in the Northwest. Jim Scribbins notes, "These sales, together with sales to other railroads, enabled rail service to continue for more than 90% of the shipments handled on Milwaukee rails west of Miles City, Montana."

Trying to Make a Profit from the Core Railroad

The key elements of the Hillman-Ogilvie plan to return the Milwaukee to profitability were:
- Paring back to a core system;
- Rehabilitating the physical plant to enable it to carry more traffic; and
- Securing new business.

Increasing a locomotive's weight increases its tractive effort, which allows it to pull more tonnage. One way of accomplishing this is with a "slug," an unpowered unit whose traction motors get their power from one or more powered units. The Milwaukee experimented with road slugs in the 1970s, as illustrated by the cut-down unit behind U30B 5604, arriving at Bensenville in November 1977. *Tom Murray*

The three steps did not necessarily progress in this order, however. Rehabilitation work on major lines had actually begun in 1977, with funds made available under the Railroad Revitalization and Regulatory Reform Act of 1976, better known as the 4R Act. Initially the Milwaukee received $4.9 million and in 1977, an additional $9.3 million in return for Redeemable Preference Shares. In an issue of *The Milwaukee Road Magazine* that went to press soon after the bankruptcy filing, the company said that the $9.3 million was being used to install "approximately 280,000 new crossties, about 15.5 miles of new welded rail, and 60 sets of new switch ties in the main line between Milwaukee and Newport, Minnesota." The article noted "the federal money isn't a gift to the Milwaukee." It would have to be paid back, with interest. Additional funding, and additional projects, would follow, not just for track rehabilitation but for car and locomotive repair as well.

In *The Milwaukee Road 1928–1985*, Scribbins writes, "from 1978 through 1983, the railroad spent $600 million on maintenance-of-way improvements. Main projects

Continued on page 138

In February 1978, Milwaukee train 240, led by GP40 2008, makes its way down the middle of the street in Bellevue, Iowa. *Joe McMillan*

Below: MILW extra 163 East exits Pipestone Pass tunnel, east of Butte, in June 1979. *Steve Glischinski*

MILW 141 and 134 are on the head end of westbound train 201, crossing Big Dick Creek Trestle in June 1979. *Phil Mason*

This August 1978 company photo by Jim Scribbins finds SD40-2 151 and U36C 5802 at Milwaukee Shops. *Milwaukee Road Archives of the Milwaukee Public Library*

were laying almost four million ties, installing 400 track miles of continuous welded rail (CWR) and more than 1,200 miles of reballasting." One Milwaukee veteran says "until that time, the Milwaukee lagged considerably behind most of the railroad industry in installing CWR, even though mainline CWR projects had been included in the railroad's annual capital improvement budgets since the 1950s. The company's financial condition simply would not allow them to take that step forward." Not only were the Milwaukee's rail and ties substandard; even its ballast, much of which was gravel, was inferior to the rock ballast used by other major railroads.

Equipment standards had changed, too. In the 1960s, Southern Railway had introduced the "Big John" 100-ton covered hopper car. It took a while for the 100-ton car to catch on with the rest of the industry, but by the early 1970s, it was superseding the 40-foot boxcar as a way of transporting grain. Richard Saunders says, "the jumbo cars did not necessarily need heavy rail, but they needed good track with sound rail joints and sound structures underneath (bridges and culverts). This meant that granger branches on, say, the Milwaukee Road or the Rock Island, which could barely roll 40-foot boxcars and could not justify the improvements for the big cars, would die."

Even if some branchlines might not be economically sustainable, the rehabilitation of its key lines allowed the Milwaukee to become competitive again in some markets, particularly in light of new and innovative labor arrangements. In early 1978, the railroad reached an agreement with the United Transportation Union that allowed it to eliminate one brakeman's position on many freight trains, with affected employees benefiting from a productivity fund. That change, plus an alteration in the standard crew district arrangements for engineers between Chicago and St. Paul, was an element in the *Sprint* intermodal service that began in June 1978.

It's June 1979 and the wires are gone, but Milwaukee train 201 is stopped at Avery for a crew change before heading west to Tacoma. Near the head end are several of the 100-ton covered hoppers that helped the Milwaukee compete for business, but hastened the deterioration of its track. *Phil Mason*

Pelletized iron ore was often loaded at Groveland Mine while still hot from processing at the plant, hence the steaming cars in this train just north of Iron Mountain, Michigan, in May 1979. The cars not steaming may have been loaded earlier, or loaded from a stockpile at the plant. *Mike Cleary*

The *Sprint* trains began as part of a Federal Railroad Administration program. They were an effort to maximize both equipment productivity and service, and to demonstrate that railroads could capture business moving by truck. There were up to three departures daily from each terminal, and trains ran on a 10-hour schedule with two hours for loading, unloading, and locomotive servicing. Thus, each set could make a roundtrip every 24 hours. The FRA provided financial assistance for the first two years, but the service was enough of a success that Milwaukee kept it going without subsidy after the demonstration period ended.

Given the competitive nature of intermodal business, its margins are thinner than most carload business. The *Sprints* may not have been a huge money-maker for the Milwaukee but they showed what the railroad could do once its physical plant was brought up to snuff. Scribbins records that their on-time performance was in the high 90-percent range.

Milwaukee SD40-2 22 was a Locotrol master unit, delivered to the railroad in 1973. Here, it leads a westbound freight at Butte, Montana, in August 1979. *Steve Patterson*

Ford was a big Milwaukee Road customer, and a carload of its pickup trucks can be seen toward the head end of train 201 at Avery in June 1979. *Phil Mason*

A more significant contribution to corporate profitability came from a voluntary coordination agreement between the Milwaukee and Grand Trunk Corporation (GTC), the U.S. subsidiary of Canadian National Railway. GTC had two operating units that connected with the Milwaukee: Grand Trunk Western at Chicago and Duluth, Winnipeg & Pacific (DW&P) at Duluth/Superior. In 1981, GTC began talking with trustee Ogilvie about a possible acquisition, which would give GTC and CN an all-U.S. route south of the Great Lakes.

The GTC arrangement proved enormously beneficial to The Milwaukee Road. New run-through trains were initiated between Port Huron, Michigan, and Bensenville, Illinois,

Many U.S. railroads painted locomotives in red, white, and blue paint schemes to celebrate the 1976 Bicentennial. The Milwaukee Road's contribution to this effort was SD40-2 No. 156, seen here on its way into Bensenville Yard in November 1975. *Tom Murray*

and between Winnipeg and St. Paul. Scribbins says that the GTC traffic was "the major reason CMStP&P had its first profitable year [1983] since 1974."

Still, the GTC agreement wasn't the only thing that had changed for the Milwaukee Road in the 1980s. In the fall of 1980, congress had passed the Staggers Act, giving railroads rate-making freedoms greater than in the past (including the ability to negotiate confidential contracts with shippers) and relaxing the standards for line sales and abandonments. The changes in the Staggers Act promoted a more entrepreneurial approach to business at the Milwaukee and throughout the rail industry. New joint-line services were one manifestation of this, such as the *Golden State Express* perishables service with Southern Pacific and Cotton Belt via Kansas City. One former Milwaukee manager says of the 1980–1985 period, "it was an exciting time!"

In May 1982, Judge Thomas McMillan gave his blessing to the GTC proposal to acquire the Milwaukee, and on April 1, 1983, Ogilvie filed an amended reorganization plan based on a GTC acquisition. But GTC's efforts to acquire The Milwaukee Road were hamstrung by a lack of financial backing from its parent company. Once other bidders for the Milwaukee emerged, the bidding quickly got too rich for GTC, and in 1984 GTW and DW&P moved much of their business to Burlington Northern.

At Green Island, Iowa, the Milwaukee route to Council Bluffs left the north-south line along the Mississippi River to go west across the Hawkeye State. A six-unit set—three GP20s and three F-units—passes Green Island tower with train 413 in May 1979.
John Leopard

The Milwaukee Road Becomes Part of Soo Line (and Canadian Pacific)

With the benefits of the GTC traffic, new marketing initiatives, and an improved physical plant, the Milwaukee began to look like a more attractive property than it had for quite some time. In July 1983, the Chicago & North Western said it would like to acquire The Milwaukee Road. It was hardly a secret that if that happened, much duplicate trackage would fall by the wayside. C&NW criticized the GTC proposal, saying that GTC was simply a surrogate for the Canadian government, which owned parent company CN. Nonsense, GTC replied: the U.S. subsidiary was expected to earn its own keep, and there was nothing in the GTC plan that would threaten Milwaukee's customers or employees.

By early 1984, another bidder, Soo Line Railroad Company, 56 percent owned by Canadian Pacific Railway, had entered the fray. Unlike C&NW, a Soo acquisition of Milwaukee would be largely end-to-end in nature, although Soo did have a Chicago–Twin Cities route of its own. Both the C&NW and Soo Line offers for Milwaukee were in the vicinity of $170 million, plus $250 million in assumption of debt, with the tax benefits of The Milwaukee Road's operating losses to stay with the trustee. GTC's offer was largely a matter of assuming the debt, plus a small amount of cash.

All three proposals went to the Interstate Commerce Commission, which because of vacancies was down to four commissioners from its normal roster of seven. In September the ICC rejected GTC's bid as financially inadequate, split evenly on C&NW's, and found in favor of Soo Line's by 3 to 1.

GTC dropped out of the bidding. C&NW upped its offer by $200 million and Ogilvie now said that he would favor this deal

Continued on page 148

The Controversial Milwaukee Road

A well-researched and dispassionate book should one day be written about the last 15 years of The Milwaukee Road's corporate existence, answering such questions as:
- Why did the people involved—management, trustees, public officials, attorneys for the parties involved, employee representatives, shippers, and officers of connecting railroads—make the decisions they did?
- Why did certain outcomes that stakeholders in the Milwaukee strove for not come to pass?
- What did The Milwaukee Road's demise as an operating railroad ultimately cost, both in hard dollars and in longer-term economic impact?

In the meantime, controversies will continue to swirl about this period of the railroad's history. Should the Milwaukee have accepted the 1970 offer of C&NW's Ben Heineman to sell his railroad to The Milwaukee Road? Was Milwaukee Road management distracted by the creation of a holding company in the early 1970s? Did Burlington Northern take actions that undercut the benefits to The Milwaukee Road of ICC-imposed merger conditions? Should the electrification have been turned off, or could it have been renewed at a reasonable cost? Should the western lines have been jettisoned, as they were, or should they have been retained as the core of a new, profitable Milwaukee?

For the most part, these issues have been addressed in Internet discussion groups and other informal forums. This book does not try to resolve these questions. In the future, followers of The Milwaukee Road may be fortunate enough to see a fully developed and well-documented analysis of this period, provided that someone with the qualifications to do so acts soon while the relevant documents are available and while at least some of those who were directly involved are still alive.

As traffic patterns changed, some yard trackage around the Milwaukee fell into disuse, and maintenance slackened. In July 1981, train 261 negotiates a yard deep in weeds at Savanna, Illinois. *John Leopard*

Above: In 1974, the Milwaukee Shops began upgrading some of the railroad's SD7s and SD9s to 1850-horsepower SD10s; eventually, the Milwaukee would roster 21 SD10s. The most notable changes cosmetically were chopped noses and yoke-type air filters. Train 420 is at Iron Mountain, Michigan, in November 1979, with three SD10s up front. *Mike Cleary* Below: Clinton, Iowa, between Sabula and Davenport, enjoyed service by four major railroads: Burlington Northern, Milwaukee, Chicago & North Western, and Rock Island. Train 399, led by former passenger unit 2 and an SD45, passes the joint BN–Rock Island freight office in March 1980. *John Leopard*

Left: Oolitic, Indiana, was known for its limestone industry, and the Milwaukee had a short branch that fed the limestone mills there. To reach the mills, the branch from Bedford crossed this trestle, which MILW SW1200 608 is maneuvering at a crawl in April 1980. *Dave Gayer* Below: The embargo of Lines West and other Milwaukee lines in February 1980 left the railroad with a large surplus of motive power; some are in evidence in January 1981 at South Minneapolis. Today this site is covered by the Metro Transit Light Rail Transit Shop. *Steve Glischinski*

The major rail-served business at Poynette, Wisconsin, on the Milwaukee's Portage–Madison line, was the Jamieson Brothers feed mill, where the crew is reboarding the locomotive in June 1981, after completing their switching activities. Power for the local is SD10 532, originally built as an SD9 in 1954. *Tom Murray*

because it rewarded the company's shareholders so much better than did the Soo Line proposal. Most observers (and C&NW itself) thought that C&NW now had the upper hand.

Judge McMillan, however, surprised virtually everyone involved when, on February 8, 1985, he awarded The Milwaukee Road's operating assets to Soo Line, saying that the anticompetitive effects of a C&NW transaction were not worth the extra benefit to The Milwaukee Road's estate. C&NW had done extensive preparation for its acquisition of Milwaukee; Soo, feeling that it was no longer in the running, had done very little.

A legal appeal by CMC was rejected, and on February 20, 1985, Soo Line Railroad Company became the owner of The Milwaukee Road's rail operating assets. Soo Line's own identity would begin to disappear within a few years as CPR first bought out the railroad's minority shareholders and then integrated it with its Canadian operations.

Operationally, those portions of the Milwaukee that became part of Soo Line now wear the "Canadian Pacific Railway" logo. In some way it is fitting that a railroad as proud of its history as The Milwaukee Road should now be part of another road that has an equally rich record of accomplishment.

CHRONOLOGY OF THE FINAL FIFTEEN YEARS

The last 15 years of the Milwaukee's existence were marked by a number of milestones and decision points, each of which influenced the events that followed:

- March 2, 1970: Burlington Northern comes into existence.

- March 22, 1971: First Milwaukee Road train arrives in Portland, under an ICC-mandated condition of the BN merger.

- May 1, 1971: Operation of Milwaukee Road's intercity passenger trains is transferred to Amtrak.

- January 14, 1972: Holding company Chicago Milwaukee Corporation becomes the owner of The Milwaukee Road, with former railroad shareholders now owning stock in CMC.

- July 15, 1972: Worthington L. Smith becomes president of The Milwaukee Road at age 47, replacing Curtiss Crippen, who retired. Smith had started his rail career with GN and was vice president of market development at BN before joining the Milwaukee.

- March 1, 1973: First Milwaukee Road train arrives in Louisville under an ICC-mandated condition of the Louisville & Nashville–Monon merger.

- March 9, 1973: Milwaukee Road petitions the ICC for inclusion in the BN merger. The ICC would reject this proposal in 1976.

- June 16, 1974: Electric operations end on The Milwaukee Road's western extension.

- April 1, 1977: Milwaukee Road trains to and from Kansas City move to a 240-mile segment of the Rock Island due to the poor condition of the Milwaukee's own line. In May 1978, they would move back to the Milwaukee route after Rock Island failed to obtain federal financial support for line rehabilitation.

- December 11, 1977: Milwaukee Road trains to and from Council Bluffs move to a 132-mile segment of the C&NW, also because of poor track conditions on the Milwaukee's own line.

- December 19, 1977: The Milwaukee Road files a voluntary bankruptcy petition, citing a worsening shortage of cash.

- January 18, 1978: Federal Judge Thomas McMillan, who would oversee the Milwaukee's bankruptcy proceeding, appoints Stanley E. G. Hillman, chairman of Illinois Central Gulf, as trustee of the railroad.

- August 3, 1978: Hillman states that in order to allow the Milwaukee to emerge from bankruptcy, it will have to abandon its routes west of the Twin Cities.

- October 1, 1978: William J. Quinn retires as CEO of The Milwaukee Road. Worthington Smith is named CEO, retaining his title as president of the railroad.

- February 7, 1979: The Association to Save Our Railroad Employment (SORE), consisting largely of employees on Milwaukee's Lines West, and which subsequently attracted the support of shippers, states, and others, proposes to convert the Twin Cities–Puget Sound route into a for-profit railroad.

- April 1979: Trustee Hillman proposes to embargo roughly three-quarters of the railroad; the court rejects his application in June.

- June 14, 1979: Trustee Hillman resigns and is replaced by former Illinois Governor Richard Ogilvie, who had been serving as counsel to the trustee.

- August 8, 1979: Trustee Ogilvie applies to abandon 2,498 route-miles west of Miles City, Montana.

SD10 532 leads the last eastbound Rapid City local through Kennebec, South Dakota, on March 1, 1980. From the photographer's notes: "The operations on these trains worked like this: one train went west from Mitchell to Murdo, South Dakota; the other came from Rapid City to Murdo. Both crews spent the night at Murdo, swapped trains, and returned to their respective terminals. This is the eastbound that left Rapid City the day before and is heading east after spending the night in Murdo." *Steve Glischinski*

Chronology, continued

- August 10, 1979: Preliminary reorganization plan is filed calling for a slimmed-down "Milwaukee II" that would operate on lines from Chicago to St. Paul and Duluth, and to Kansas City and Louisville.

- November 2, 1979: Congress passes Milwaukee Road Restructuring Act, giving bankruptcy court power over lines sales, transfers, and abandonments, and providing $75 million for employee protection.

- February 29, 1980: Embargo takes effect on lines in western Montana, Idaho, and Washington, as well as certain lines in North Dakota, South Dakota, and Iowa.

- March 15, 1980: Last train departs east from Tacoma.

- March 19, 1980: ICC rejects the trustee's reorganization plan as well as the former SORE (now New Milwaukee Lines) plan and the plan (supported by CMC) for liquidation of the railroad.

- May 27, 1980: First sale of a portion of the western extension occurs (Avery–St. Maries, Idaho, sold to Potlatch Corporation for private rail operation).

- June 1980: Court approves abandonment of line from Green Island, Iowa, to Council Bluffs.

- October 1980: Staggers Rail Act reduces regulation of U.S. railroads, and provides forgiveness of $60 million in Milwaukee Road financial obligations to federal government once 50 percent of the railroad is sold and 50 percent of its employees have obtained jobs with other railroads.

- November 1980: South Dakota acquires 764 route-miles of Milwaukee for $18.75 million.

- March 1981: BN acquires former Milwaukee Road segments in Washington, Montana, South Dakota, North Dakota, and Minnesota.

- September 15, 1981: Trustee Ogilvie files a new reorganization plan providing for a 2,800-mile railroad, with profitability expected in 1983.

- September 24, 1981: South Dakota legislature approves a plan to purchase the Ortonville (Minnesota)–Terry (Montana) Line for $30 million, to be leased to BN so that coal train operations to Ottertail Power can continue.

- October 27, 1981: Grand Trunk Corporation (U.S. unit of Canadian National Railway) and Milwaukee announce that they are considering a plan whereby GTC would acquire Milwaukee II. CN and GTC have already begun to route certain traffic over The Milwaukee Road between Duluth and Chicago, as well as the high-revenue auto parts business from Chicago to Kansas City. The Voluntary Coordination Agreement with GTC would produce substantial volumes of business for the Milwaukee until terminated in 1984.

- April 19, 1982: Sale of Ortonville–Terry Line to state of South Dakota is completed and BN begins operations on April 20.

- April 1, 1983: Trustee files amended reorganization plan calling for sale of Milwaukee II to GTC.

- July 22, 1983: C&NW says it will make an offer to buy The Milwaukee Road.

- February 17, 1984: Soo Line Railroad Company applies to court to acquire operating assets of the Milwaukee. Soo's plan provides for continued operation of most Milwaukee II lines.

- April 6, 1984: Bidding war between C&NW and Soo Line begins. Soo increases its bid to $168 million (from $40 million), and C&NW to $170 million (from $60 million). Both would also assume $250 million in debt and leave tax benefits with the trustee. GTC's offer is approximately $160 million less than C&NW's.

- September 26, 1984: ICC approves Soo proposal 3 to 1, but is evenly split on C&NW proposal. GTC proposal is rejected as financially inadequate.

- October 1984: C&NW increases its bid by $210 million.

Milwaukee train 223 from Kansas City to St. Paul negotiates the street trackage of Bellevue, Iowa, on February 18, 1985. The following day, Judge Thomas McMillan would surprise many with his order awarding the Milwaukee to bidder Soo Line, rather than to Chicago & North Western. This line is now part of the Iowa, Chicago & Eastern Railroad. *Steve Glischinski*

Chronology, continued

- December 20, 1984: ICC approves C&NW's offer by 5 to 2, and Soo's by 4 to 3. The commission finds that the Soo proposal, while lower than C&NW's, is less likely to result in line abandonments and closing of duplicate facilities.

- February 8, 1985: With the Soo Line's financial offer standing at a total of $570 million, and the C&NW's at $780 million, Judge McMillan approves the Soo Line's offer. He finds that a sale to C&NW would defeat "a substantial amount of competition." C&NW withdraws its offer. CMC seeks an order to prevent Judge McMillan's order from being carried out, but the U.S. Court of Appeals for the Seventh Circuit denies this request.

- February 19, 1985: Judge McMillan enters an order authorizing Soo's acquisition of The Milwaukee Road's operating assets. Trustee Ogilvie and Soo President Dennis M. Cavanaugh sign the legal documents making the sale effective.

- February 28, 1985: Soo Line creates a new subsidiary, The Milwaukee Road, Inc., as the legal owner of the assets purchased from the trustee.

- December 31, 1985: The Milwaukee Road, Inc. is fully merged into the Soo Line Railroad.

This chronology relies to a great degree on Jim Scribbins' *The Milwaukee Road 1928–1985*. Anyone wishing to become better informed about this period would do well to start with the relevant chapters of this book. Its author worked for The Milwaukee Road from 1948 to 1985, and served on the company's public relations staff during its final decade.

Soo Line obliterated the words "Milwaukee" and "Milwaukee Road" from locomotives and other equipment as expeditiously as possible after taking ownership of The Milwaukee Road in February 1985. Some former Milwaukee employees, however, did their best to postpone the loss of identity from the 37 locomotives that bore the revived *Hiawatha* image. Here, MILW 189, one of the repainted SD40-2s, leads train 261 across the Mississippi River into Sabula, Iowa, in September 1986. *John Leopard*

Train 602, known by train crews as the "Big I&M" local, is at Mendota, Minnesota, en route from St. Paul to Austin, Minnesota, on September 30, 1984. On the head end is SDL39 586, a Milwaukee-only version of EMD's SD39 locomotive, designed to safely negotiate weight-restricted track and bridges. There were two trains out of St. Paul on the I&M (Iowa & Minnesota) line. One was a local that ran between St. Paul and Rosemount (the "Little I&M") and the other was the through train to Austin (the "Big I&M"). *Steve Glischinski*

Train 221 was a Bensenville–Kansas City run, with traffic destined for Union Pacific, and locomotives would often run through from one railroad to the other. That explains why UP 2480 is trailing MILW SD40-2 141 as its passes West Davenport, Iowa, in July 1982. At this point, The Milwaukee Road came off the Davenport, Rock Island & North Western from Clinton and began 26 miles of trackage rights over the Rock Island to Culver Tower at Muscatine, Iowa, where Milwaukee trains regained their own track toward Kansas City. *John Leopard*

It's September 1986, more than a year-and-a-half since The Milwaukee Road came under the ownership of Soo Line Railroad Company. At Savanna, Illinois, SD40-2s of both lineages keep company. *John Leopard*

The Milwaukee operated unit coal trains from Gascoyne, North Dakota, to an Ottertail Power generating station at Big Stone City, South Dakota. On March 27, 1982, the empty westbound train is seen at Bristol, South Dakota, en route back to the mine. The covers on the cars were designed to keep the soft lignite coal dry during the rail trip, and to eliminate blowoff of coal fines. On April 1, 1982, this portion of the railroad was taken over by Burlington Northern. The line from Ortonville, Minnesota, to Terry, Montana, was purchased by the state of South Dakota for just over $30 million on July 20, 1982. BN was given the right to purchase the line and eventually did so. *Steve Glischinski*

Epilogue: The Legacy of The Milwaukee Road

You can't ride a Milwaukee Road train any longer, and the company's famous tilted-rectangle red logo has largely disappeared.

However, there are many people still working in the rail industry who got their start with The Milwaukee Road. They help carry on the tradition of a railroad whose scrappy way of doing business kept it alive despite the adversities of nature, the aggressiveness of some of its competitors, and the precariousness of its finances.

The physical legacy of The Milwaukee Road will survive even longer than will its roster of alumni in the railroad industry, as traffic continues to move over rights-of-way once part of this proud and independent railroad. After it acquired the assets of the Milwaukee in 1985, the Soo Line (now Canadian Pacific) quickly jettisoned its original route between Chicago and the Twin Cities in favor of The Milwaukee Road's faster, higher-capacity route. Other former Milwaukee Road routes survive as part of Burlington Northern Santa Fe; Iowa, Chicago & Eastern; Twin Cities & Western; and other railroads. In the Chicago area, former Milwaukee routes to Fox Lake and Elgin are key parts of the Metra commuter rail system.

Although they operate today under a variety of ownerships, the routes of The Milwaukee Road continue to play an important role in North American rail transportation.

The early 1980s were a period of resurgence for The Milwaukee Road. Track rehabilitation and interline agreements with other railroads helped bring traffic back to the railroad. To symbolize the pride that many in the company felt in this turnaround, the *Hiawatha* logo was brought back as one element in a revamped locomotive paint scheme. MILW 130, shown here at Bensenville, Illinois, in June 1984, was one of 37 units to receive the new paint scheme. *Eric Blasko*

SOURCES

Books

Derleth, August. *The Milwaukee Road: Its First Hundred Years.* Iowa City, Iowa: Univ. of Iowa Press, 2002.

Dubin, Arthur D. *More Classic Trains.* Milwaukee, Wis.: Kalmbach Publishing Co., 1974.

Holley, Noel T. *The Milwaukee Electrics.* Mukilteo, Wash.: Hundman Publishing, Inc., 2002.

Middleton, William. *When the Steam Railroads Electrified.* Milwaukee, Wis.: Kalmbach Publishing Co., 1974.

Ploss, Thomas H. *The Nation Pays Again.* N.p.: T. H. Ploss, 1984.

Saunders, Richard. *Main Lines: North American Railroads 1900–1970.* DeKalb, Ill.: Northern Illinois Univ. Press, 2001.

——. *Merging Lines Lines: Rebirth of the North American Railroads 1970–2002.* DeKalb, Ill.: Northern Illinois Univ. Press, 2003.

Schwantes, Carlos A. *Railroad Signatures across the Pacific Northwest.* Seattle: Univ. of Washington Press, 1993.

Scribbins, Jim. *The Hiawatha Story.* Milwaukee, Wis.: Kalmbach Publishing Co., 1970.

——. *Milwaukee Road In Its Hometown.* Waukesha, Wis.: Kalmbach Publishing Co., 1998.

——. *Milwaukee Road Remembered.* Waukesha, Wis.: Kalmbach Publishing Co., 1990.

——. *The Milwaukee Road 1928–1985.* Forest Park, Ill.: Heimberger House Publishing Co., 2001.

Wood, Charles R. and Dorothy M. Wood. *Milwaukee Road West.* Seattle: Superior Publishing Co., 1972.

Other Publications

Anderson, Robert C. and Dick Will. "Milwaukee Road Diesel Locomotive Roster." *Extra 2200 South: The Locomotive Newsmagazine*, Vol. 9, No. 1, July 1971.

Cummings, Doug E., Ken L. Douglas and Dick Will. "Milwaukee Road Electric Locomotive Roster." *Extra 2200 South: The Locomotive Newsmagazine*, Vol. 9, No. 3, Jan. 1972.

Edson, W. D. "Milwaukee Road Locomotives: All Time Steam, Diesel and Electric Roster." *Railroad History*, Issue 136, Spring 1977.

Milwaukee Road Historical Association. *The Milwaukee Railroader*, various issues.

Moody's Investors Service, *Manual of Investments: Railroad Securities*, various editions.

——. *Transportation Manual*, various editions.

The Official Guide of the Railways, various issues. New York: National Railway Publication Company.

Schmidt, W. H. "The Singular Milwaukee: A Profile." *Railroad History*, Issue 136, Spring 1977.

Specht, Ray. "The Milwaukee and Northern." *Railroad History*, Issue 121, Oct. 1969.

TRAINS Magazine, various issues. Milwaukee and Waukesha, Wis.: Kalmbach Publishing Co.

Wilkerson, Bill. *Milwaukee Diesels 1929–1985.* Harlowton, Mont.: *The Times Clarion*, undated.

Company Materials

Annual Reports, Chicago Milwaukee Corporation, 1971–1978.

Annual Reports, Chicago, Milwaukee & St. Paul Railway Company, 1881–1924.

Annual Reports, Chicago, Milwaukee, St. Paul & Pacific Railroad Company, 1928–1970.

Brief Record of the Development of The Milwaukee Road, 1939 and 1944 editions.

Maps and Travel Brochures, various dates.

The Milwaukee Electrification: A Proud Era Passes, prepared by the Public Relations Department of the Chicago, Milwaukee, St. Paul and Pacific Railroad Company as a special supplement to the July-Aug. 1973 issue of *The Milwaukee Road Magazine*.

The Milwaukee Road Magazine, various issues.

The Milwaukee Road: A Brief History, 1968.

Public and employee timetables, various dates.

Statistics of Operation, Chicago, Milwaukee & St. Paul Railway, 1925–1927.

Other Resources

Abbey, Wally. "Restructuring the Milwaukee Road: A discussion at 'Midwest Rail, Restructuring for the 1980s,'" University of Wisconsin Extension Division of Urban Outreach, Madison, Wis. June 16, 1980. Private manuscript

Chicago, Milwaukee, St. Paul and Pacific Railroad Company, et al., Petitioners v. United States of America, et al., No. 86-1234, In the Supreme Court of the United States, October Term, 1986, On Petition for a Writ of Certiorari to the United States Court of Appeals for the Seventh Circuit, Brief for the Respondents in Opposition, http://www.usdoj.gov/osg/briefs/1986/sg860073.txt

Jones, Todd: "Milwaukee Road in the 70's: What really happened?" http://www.trainweb.org/milwaukee/article.html

Milwaukee Road All-time Diesel Roster, 1939–1993, Compiled by Fred Hyde, http://www.trainweb.org/milwaukee/roster.txt

Milwaukee Road Historical Association web site, http://mrha.com

Yahoo! Groups: MILW (A historical discussion list for fans and modelers of the Chicago, Milwaukee, St. Paul & Pacific Railroad), http://finance.groups.yahoo.com/group/MILW

INDEX

400, 86, 87
4R Act, 135
744th Railway Operating Battalion, 63
Abraham Lincoln, 122
Afternoon Hiawathas, 86, 90, 92, 94
Air Line Yard, Milwaukee, 101, 103
American Locomotive Company (Alco), 44, 67, 70, 71, 73, 88, 102, 104
American Railway Union, 29
Amtrak, 90, 94, 122
Anaconda Copper Mining Company, 38, 42, 44
Armour, Phillip, 31
Army Transportation Corps, 63
Arrow, 81, 92
Association of American Railroads, 97
Association to Save Our Railroad Employment (SORE), 134, 149, 151
Baldwin Locomotive Works, 69, 70
Baltimore & Ohio Chicago Terminal Company, 48
Bensenville Yard, Illinois, 72, 103, 127, 135, 143, 157
"Big I&M", 154
"Bi-Polar" locomotives, 34, 44, 80
Black River Junction, 40, 44
Brotherhood of Locomotive Engineers, 64
Brotherhood of Railroad Trainmen, 64
Brundage, Edward J., 51
Budd Company, 87
Buford, Charles H., 97, 98, 110, 118
Burlington Northern (BN), 11, 54, 104, 110, 118, 122, 128–131, 143, 145, 146, 149, 151, 156
Burlington Northern Santa Fe, 156
Butte, Anaconda & Pacific, 38, 44
Byram, Harry E., 45, 48, 51, 54
Calmar-to-Lawler line, 19
Canadian National Railway, 10, 142, 144, 151
Canadian Pacific Railway (CPR), 36, 124, 144, 148, 156
Cavanaugh, Dennis M., 153
Cedar Falls–Monroe Line, 118

Cedar Rapids, 86
Centralized Traffic Control (CTC), 64, 104
Challenger, 92, 94
Chicago & North Western (C&NW), 10, 18, 22, 36, 56, 86, 87, 89, 93, 94, 96, 109, 110, 112, 114, 118, 119, 130, 131, 144–146, 148, 151–153
Chicago American, 56
Chicago Great Western, 93
Chicago Milwaukee Corporation (CMC), 127, 148, 149, 151, 153
Chicago Transit Authority, 80
"Chicago Railroad Fair", 85
Chicago, Burlington & Quincy (CB&Q), 11, 34, 37, 52, 86, 87, 89, 93, 94, 110, 116, 118, 119
Chicago, Milwaukee & Gary Railway, 48, 50
Chicago, Milwaukee & Puget Sound, 33, 44
Chicago, Milwaukee & St. Paul Railway Company, founding, 22, 24
Chicago, Milwaukee, St. Paul & Pacific Railroads Company, founding, 53
Chicago, North Shore & Milwaukee Railway, 80
Chicago, Rock Island & Pacific (CRI&P), 93, 110, 118, 119, 121, 139, 146, 149
Chicago, Terre Haute & Southeastern Railway Company (CTH&SE), 48–50, 98
Chippewa, 92
Chippew-Hiawatha, 92
City of Everywhere, 94, 95
City of lines, 94, 95
Columbian, 38, 81, 83, 84
Conrail, 121, 124
Cooke Locomotive Works, 23
Copper Country Limited, 81, 89, 92
Council Bluffs Line, 134
Crippen, Curtiss E., 118, 149
CSX, 124
Dakota Rail, Inc., 12
Davenport, Rock Island & North Western Railway, 52
Day Express, 89

Debs, Eugene V., 29
Delaware & Hudson, 109
Depression, 55
Derleth, August, 16, 17, 21, 23, 24, 29, 34, 38, 45, 48, 53, 56
Dubin, Arthur, 82, 83, 87
Duluth, Winnipeg & Pacific (DW&P), 142, 143
Earling, Albert J., 32, 45
Edson, William D., 65
Eisenhower, Dwight D., 106
Electrification, 42, 44, 45
Electro-Motive Division, 70, 71, 73
Electro-Motive plant, 58
Erie, 109
Escanaba & Lake Superior Railroad, 112
Fairbanks-Morse, 82, 83, 85, 116
Federal Highway Act, 106
Federal Railroad Administration, 139, 140
Flexi-van, 110
Flynn, George, 56
Gallatin Gateway Inn, 87
General Electric Company, 39, 44, 63, 69, 70, 83, 119, 128, 134
General Motors, 62, 73
Glischinski, Steve, 55
Golden State Express, 143
Grand Trunk Corporation (GTC), 142–144, 151
Grand Trunk Western (GTW), 10, 142, 143
Grange movement, 23
Grant Locomotive Works, 16
Great Northern (GN), 8, 11, 32, 34, 37, 40, 45, 110, 116, 118, 119, 125, 149
Greater Lake County Mass Transit District, 125
Green Bay & Western, 54
Groveland Mine run, 112, 115, 130, 140
Grube, John, 74
Gulf, Mobile & Ohio, 122
Harriman, E. H., 31, 34
Hastings, Philip, 72
Heinemann, Ben, 131, 145

Hiawatha Story, The, 89
Hiawathas, 7, 15, 67, 68, 82, 86–91, 153, 157
Hill, James J., 31, 32, 34, 125
Hill lines, 8, 11, 34, 42
Hillman, Stanley, 134, 149
Holley, Noel T., 34
Illinois Central, 36, 93, 110, 149
Indiana Harbor Belt (IHB), 124
Indiana Line, 98
Interstate Commerce Commission (ICC), 50, 54, 56, 63, 108, 118, 129–131, 134, 144, 145, 149, 151, 153
Iowa & Minnesota Line (I&M), 154
Iowa, Chicago & Eastern Railroad, 152, 156
Kansas City Southern Railway, 63
Kilbourn, Byron, 16, 17, 20
Kiley, John P., 98, 110, 118
"King of the Rails" Bi-Polar, 35
Kuhn, Loeb & Company, 53
Lackawanna, 109
La Crosse & Milwaukee, 17, 18, 20, 24
Lines West, 120, 129, 134, 149
"Little I&M", 154
Little Joes, 105–109, 111, 113, 123, 124
Loewy, Raymond, 83
Louisville & Nashville, 51, 109, 130, 131, 149
Marion Junction, 22
Marquette, 92
McMillan, Thomas, 143, 148, 149, 152, 153
Menomonee Foundry, Milwaukee, 17
Merging Lines: American Railroads 1900–1970, 93
Merrill, S. S., 24
Metra Milwaukee District, 127
Metra, 127
Metro Transit Light Rail Transit Stop, 147
Middleton, William D., 44
Midwest Hiawatha, 91–93
Miller, Roswell, 24
Milton Junction, 18
Milwaukee & Mississippi Railroad Company (M&M), 15–20, 22, 24, 98
Milwaukee & Northern Railroad Company (M&N), 28, 29, 82
Milwaukee & Prairie du Chien Railway Company, 18, 21, 24
Milwaukee & St. Paul Railway (M&StP), 20–22, 24
Milwaukee & Waukesha Railroad Company, 15, 98
Milwaukee Depot, 70
Milwaukee Electrics, The, 34
"Milwaukee" fleet, 65–67
Milwaukee Land Company, 24
Milwaukee Magazine, The, 56
Milwaukee Railroader, The, 55, 56, 85
Milwaukee Road 1928–1985, The, 72, 101, 135, 153
Milwaukee Road, Inc., The, founding, 153
Milwaukee Road Magazine, The, 135
Milwaukee Road Remembered, 66, 78, 84
Milwaukee Road Restructuring Act, 151
Milwaukee Road West, 40
Milwaukee Sentinel, 24
Milwaukee Shops, 60, 64, 66, 71, 73–75, 82, 83, 98, 100, 101, 113, 117, 138, 146
Milwaukee-Kansas City Southern yard, 104

Minneapolis & St. Louis (M&StL), 110, 118
Minneapolis, St. Paul & Sault Ste. Marie (Soo Line), 36, 110
Mitchell, Alexander, 19–25
Monon, 130, 149
Montana Line, 12
Montana Power Company, 42, 44
Montana Railroad "Jawbone line", 38
Moody's Transportation Manual, 104, 114, 118
More Classic Trains, 82
Morgan, J. P., 31, 32, 34
Morning Hiawatha, 68, 73, 89, 90
Nashville, Chattanooga & Salt Lake, 109
Nation Pays Again, The, 129
National City Bank, 53
New Haven, 109
New York Central, 110, 124
Norfolk Southern, 124
North Line, 125, 127
North Suburban Mass Transit District, 125
North Woods Hiawatha, 91, 92
Northeastern Illinois Railroad Company (NIRC), 127
Northern Lines, 110, 118
Northern Pacific (NP), 8, 11, 28, 32, 34, 37, 38, 40, 45, 110, 116, 118, 119, 129
Northern Securities Corporation, 34
Northtown Yard, Minneapolis, 104
Northwest Industries, 131
Northwest Suburban Mass Transit District, 125
Ogilvie, Richard, 134, 142–144, 149, 151, 153
Olympian, 34, 38, 39, 56, 80, 82–87
Olympian Hiawatha, 10, 82, 84, 85, 122
Omaha Line, 94
On Wisconsin, 92
Oregon-Washington Railroad & Navigation Company, 42
Orton–Terry Line, 151
Ottertail Power, 151, 156
Pacific Guard, 76
Pacific Limited, 82
Panama Canal, 36, 45, 50
Panic of 1857, 17, 19
Panic of 1893, 28
Penn Central, 124
Pioneer Limited, 78, 92
Pipestone Pass, Montana, 26, 136
Ploss, Tom, 129
Plummer Junction, 42
Potlatch Corporation, 151
Potter, Mark W., 51
Potter Law, 23
Prairie State, 122
Puget Sound Line, 7, 30, 36–38, 45, 48, 67, 83, 132, 134, 149
Pullman Company, 29, 76, 83, 84
Quinn, William J., 110, 118, 131, 149
Racine & Southwestern Division, 116
Railroad History, 31, 65
Railroad Revitalization and Regulatory Reform Act of 1976, 135
Railroad Signatures Across the Pacific Northwest, 37
Reconstruction Finance Corporation, 55
Regional Transportation Authority (RTA), 125, 127
Rockefeller, William, 31, 34
Roosevelt, Theodore, 34

Ryan, John D., 42, 44
Sabula Junction, 22
Santa Fe, 94
Saunders, Richard, 93, 109, 138
Scandrett, Henry A., 54, 97
Schmidt, W. H., Jr., 31
Schwantes, Carlos A., 37, 38, 42
Scribbons, Jim, 66, 67, 72, 78, 84, 87–91, 101–103, 112, 129, 132, 134, 135, 138, 140, 153
Sioux, 92
Sisseton Line Association, 12
Sisseton Southern Railway, 12
Sisseton-Milbank Railroad, 12
Skytop Lounge, 85, 86, 90
Smith, A. O., 127
Smith, Worthington L., 149
Snoqualmie Pass, 37
Sol, Michael, 24
Soo Line Railroad Company, 11, 89, 121, 144, 148, 151–153, 155, 156
SORE, *see* Association to Save Our Railroad Employment
South Minneapolis Yard, 123
Southern Pacific, 82, 128, 143
Southern Railway, 130, 138
Southwest, 82
Southwest Limited, 92
Spokane Line, 42
Spokane, Portland & Seattle (SP&S), 11, 110, 118
Sprint, 139, 140
St. Paul & Chicago Railway Company, 22, 25
St. Paul Pass Tunnel, 7, 37
St. Paul Yard, 104, 116
Staggers Act, 143, 151
Stevens, Brooks, 82, 85
Stevens, John F., 36
The Empire Builder, 122
"The Fast Mail Line", 78
Thunderhawk, 113, 128
Tomahawk, 113, 128
Trailer-on-flatcar (TOFC), 110, 111, 114
TRAINS Magazine, 70, 73
Twin Cities & Western, 156
Twin Zephyrs, 87
U.S. Railroad Administration (USRA), 48, 50
Union Pacific, 24, 28, 34, 36, 42, 54, 76, 79, 82, 91–95, 122, 155
Union Passenger Station, Omaha, 24
Union Station, 96
United Transportation Union, 139
Varsity, 92
Viroqua Branch, 102
Wabash, 93
War Production Board, 60, 74
Waterloo, Cedar Falls & Northern, 100
West Line, 125, 127
Western Avenue coach yard, 86
Westinghouse, 39
When the Steam Railroads Electrified, 44
Whitcomb, 70
Wilkerson, Bill, 69
Wisconsin Valley Line, 46
Wood, Charles R., 40
Wood, Dorothy M., 40
XL Special, 113, 128
Zephyr, 87